KING'S CROSS LINESIDE

1958~1984

David Percival

LONDON

IAN ALLAN LTD

Contents

First published 1984

ISBN 0 7110 1380 2

Published by Ian Allan Ltd, Shepperton, Surrey;
and printed by Ian Allan Printing Ltd at their works
at Coombelands in Runnymede, England.

Introduction

The past quarter of a century has seen unpre-
cedented changes on the railways of Britain. In few
areas has the scene altered more completely than
that viewed from the lineside out of King's Cross,
where a traditional steam railway has developed into
a modern, mostly electrified, suburban system from
which springs one of the world's fastest express
passenger main line routes.

I have defined the King's Cross area — not too
arbitrarily, I believe — as the East Coast Main Line
and its former Great Northern branches, as far north
as Huntingdon. Within the limited confines of this
book I have attempted to chronicle the changes and
events that would have been observed by anyone
travelling on or familiar with the railway.

Most of the observations are from my own con-
temporary records and from those of Stevenage
Locomotive Society members, upon whose monthly
magazine I have drawn extensively. My own connection with the railways of the area is through living
within sight of the line at Knebworth and Stevenage
during the past 25 years and commuting between those
two stations or to King's Cross for almost the entire
period.

During my research I realised how much I am
indebted to all those people who reported events to
railway periodicals and to a number of railwaymen
among my friends and acquaintances whose infor-
mation over the years has enabled me to confirm or
fill gaps in my own records. My thanks, too, to the
photographers who allowed me to browse through
their collections or scoured their files for something I
specifically requested. As a result I have been able to
include many previously unpublished photographs.

The writing of this book has recalled for me many
half-forgotten scenes and half-remembered events. I
hope the reading of it will have the same effect upon
others.

Stevenage   *David Percival*
January 1984

1

The Diesels Arrive

Diesel locomotives began working in the King's Cross area in the early 1950s, in the form of a handful of 350bhp shunters, built by British Railways to an LMS design. At the start of 1958, No 12112 was based at King's Cross and Nos 12129/31/7/8 were at Hornsey. From this type was developed the standard English Electric-engined shunter (later Class 08), of which Hornsey had No 13332 while Nos 13307-12/25/31/4/6 were at King's Cross. Examples of a now-extinct variety with Blackstone engines, Nos 13161-7, were also based at the latter depot and similarly-engined Nos D3439-44/50/73-8/90 were being delivered. Within a year or two, however, all the 'Blackstones' had been transferred away in favour of new arrivals Nos D3687-93 and D3704-6/8-18/22-5.

The first standard 204bhp shunters, Nos D2000-3 (later Class 03), were delivered to King's Cross in December 1957 and redistributed to Hatfield and Hitchin sheds.

Most main line diesels built under the 1955 Modernisation Plan initially had to find accommodation at a steam locomotive shed and, for those of the King's Cross area, the chosen depot was Hornsey. The first to arrive was the English Electric 2,000bhp Type 4 (Class 40) Nos D201/6-9, in the summer of 1958. Their coming was heralded by a test trip for Stratford's No D200 from Doncaster to Welwyn Garden City and back on 9 April. The Type 4s' regular workings during the early months were undemanding, since they were mainly employed on secondary duties for crew training. Within a few days of arriving, however, No D201 gave a foretaste of things to come when it worked a Pullman timing trial from Sheffield to King's Cross on 29 April. On Saturday 21 June the same locomotive took the first diesel-hauled 'Flying Scotsman' out of the 'Cross'. It was another two months before the new machine was really stretched. On Mondays-Fridays from 25 August until 12 September a Type 4 worked the 4pm 'Talisman' to Newcastle and returned with the 'Aberdonian' sleeper. On all but the final day, No D207 was employed.

At the start of the winter 1958/9 timetable, five intensive diagrams were introduced for the Type 4s; four covered some 4,600 miles each week and the fifth a little less. Fourteen important trains were included, mostly between London and Newcastle — among them the 'Tees-Tyne Pullman' and down 'Flying Scotsman' — plus two new daily Sheffield Pullman workings in each direction.

On the suburban front, 21 August 1958 saw the arrival of Hornsey's first Type 2, the BRCW/Sulzer 1,160bhp Bo-Bo (later Class 26) No D5300. Like the North British Type 2s which came later, the type was destined for the Scottish Region but helped launch the suburban diesel service pending the arrival of Brush Type 2s.

Cravens diesel multiple-units made their first visit on 1 August (see chapter 6); the transfer of some of these units to Cambridge and the delivery of more BRCWs allowed some inner suburban services to be taken over by diesel traction during the autumn.

By early February 1959 it was possible to extend diesel working to about one third of the outer suburban service; completion of the BRCW 'pilot' series, Nos D5300-19, saw more diagrams introduced on 23 March.

From mid-February the Eastern Region had the 3,300bhp prototype *Deltic* on loan, having ordered a production series of 22 the previous April. *Deltic* was put to work on the 8.20am to Doncaster and 1.35pm (12.20pm from Hull) return. In mid-March a series of timing and braking trials took place, including a 350ton train on 16 March to Newcastle, reached in a net 3hr 50min; the fastest express at the time took $4\frac{1}{2}$hr. Five days later *Deltic* headed a 1,500ton train formed of a Dynamometer Car, 50 loaded Minfits and a brake van from Doncaster to East Goods, Finsbury Park. In the summer timetable, *Deltic* gained a second daily working to Doncaster — on the 8.20pm Edinburgh 'mail' and an up overnight

Above:
English Electric Type 4 No D201, the first main line diesel to be allocated to the King's Cross area, stands in the terminus after arriving with the 9.55am from Newcastle on 31 January 1959. *M. Mensing*

Below:
Cravens units began work on inner suburban services in the autumn of 1958. Still with a plain front end, a unit arrives at Palmers Green with a down Hertford train on 23 October. And that *must* be a hula-hoop!
BR, Eastern Region

parcels — and its morning departure was altered to the 8.50am 'White Rose'.

During the spring of 1959 the next two Type 2s began to arrive. These were the first 10 North British 1,000bhp locomotives (later Class 21) Nos D6100-9 and the English Electric 1,100bhp 'Baby Deltics' (Class 23). The latter, Nos D5900-9, were intended for use on Hertford line stopping trains (for which their rapid acceleration would have been ideal) and cross-London freight duties. In spite of modifications made before delivery to reduce weight they were not acceptable to the Southern Region, so they were based at Hitchin and spent their days almost entirely on outer suburban passenger duties.

The arrival of these Type 2s was none too soon. Such was the shortage of motive power that Stratford Brush Type 2s Nos D5503 and D5500 were borrowed to work the 5pm to Grantham on 9 and 10 April, respectively. Two other locomotives to appear at Hornsey, at the beginning of May, were English Electric 500bhp 0-6-0s, the diesel-electric No D226 (now preserved on the Keighley & Worth Valley Railway) and the diesel-hydraulic No D227. The SR would not allow them to be tried on cross-London freights as planned, and they quickly moved on to Stratford.

A major revision of the suburban timetable took place in June 1959, when quadrupling of the section through Hadley Wood and Potters Bar was completed. Most trains were now diesel powered, but reliability of the new form of traction was, to say the least, disappointing. Failures en route were frequent — especially of the NBL locomotives — and some unlucky commuters were affected almost daily by trouble with their train or a preceding one. Before long, stations in the area displayed printed notices apologising for the delays and assuring travellers that 'everything possible' was being done to rectify the problems. As a temporary expedient, Nos D5330-35 of a later batch of BRCWs were loaned to Hornsey for two months from the end of July. The 10 NBL locomotives were also joined by a later variant; No D6126, with a 1,100bhp engine, was transferred from Ipswich in October and remained for three months.

On the main line, the Type 4s were still suffering from teething troubles and on 17 September the down 'Master Cutler' fell victim to the failure of No D201 at New Barnet and its replacement, No D206, at Sandy. The arrival of No D248 early in December provided a much-needed spare locomotive for the five diagrams.

At 9am on 20 June 1960, Brush Type 2 No D5592 has brought a commuter service into Moorgate; Fowler 2-6-2T No 40033 has arrived on a similar train from the St Pancras line. *C. T. Gifford*

Two new types of diesel entered the scene at the end of the year. Starting in October, English Electric Type 1s (Class 20) Nos D8020-7/45-9 were delivered, and the 'J6s' were among the first to become redundant as the newcomers took over their local freight duties. Two months later Hornsey received Brush Type 2s Nos D5565-9, taken from a batch being delivered to the Great Eastern section. Almost immediately they were pressed into use on Christmas 'extras'; their employment in this manner was a feature of most holiday periods for the next few years. The main batch (Nos D5586-D5615) was delivered between February and May 1960, followed by Nos D5639-54 in August/September and Nos D5672-9 in November/December. As their numbers increased, the North British Type 2s were, not surprisingly, the first of the other types to go — but only as far as Peterborough. There they remained for several weeks until the Scottish Region accepted them — but not before the presence of expensive equipment lying idle had been revealed by Fleet Street. At the end of March, Nos D5565-9 went to the GE and in mid-April the BRCW Type 2s began

Below:
Below:

On one of its first workings, Brush prototype No D0280 *Falcon* passes Finsbury Park with the 1.5pm down 'Cambridge Buffet Express' on 17 October 1961.
J. F. Aylard

Bottom:

Brush Type 4 No D1508 heads one of the newly introduced New England-Ferme Park '7-star' heavy freights — comprising 70 wagons and a brake van — at Knebworth on 25 May 1963. *David Percival*

The original Type 2s which launched the suburban diesel service in 1959. *Top left:* **the BRCW version, represented by No D5317 with an up 'Cambridge Buffet Express' at Hitchin on 3 June 1960.** *Left:* **No D6104 of the unsuccessful NBL type waits to haul ECS out of King's Cross on 7 August 1959.** *Below left:* **'Baby Deltic' No D5908 passes New Southgate with the 12.51pm for Biggleswade on 21 October 1961.** *Michael Joyce (2); M. Mensing*

Above:
Standard 204bhp shunter No D2002 on duty in the up yard at Welwyn Garden City on 20 May 1959. *N. Caplan*

to head north, normally in pairs on the same day as two new Brush Type 2s arrived.

A major development in April was the opening of Finsbury Park diesel depot, which took over responsibility for maintenance of all diesel locomotives allocated to the area. Also in the spring, EE Type 1s found themselves working in emergency on the fast Cambridge passenger services and regularly on a Hitchin-Huntingdon 'local'. Over the next few years they proved themselves capable of working suburban passenger turns during the summer months when their lack of a train-heating boiler was no handicap.

The beginning of May 1960 saw the introduction of Gateshead-based EE Type 4s (Nos D237-49/70-74) on diagrams to King's Cross. Three seven-day rosters each comprised eight return trips (4,608 miles) covering King's Cross arrivals at 2.55am, 6.20am, 1pm (the fast 7.56am from Newcastle) and 9.07pm 'Heart of Midlothian', and departures at 9am, 11am, 4pm 'Talisman' and 11.35pm 'Night Scotsman'.

The variety at Finsbury Park increased late in 1960 when a handful of Paxman Type 1s (Class 15), Nos D8210/37-43 arrived for light freight duties. And in the early months of 1961 the search

for a Type 2 suitable for cross-London freight working ended successfully when BR/Sulzer Type 2s (Class 24) Nos D5050-72/94/5 came from the GE in exchange for a number of Brush Type 2s.

After working on the ECML for almost two years, the prototype *Deltic* ended its stint towards the end of 1960, a few weeks before the first production example was seen in London. Although No D9001 travelled up the main line on its way to Stratford for inspection on 17 January 1961 it was not until early March that it was delivered to Finsbury Park — the first of the depot's allocation of eight. As yet un-named, it began to earn its keep on the former *Deltic* diagram — a twice-daily return trip to Doncaster.

Finsbury Park's third 'Deltic', No D9007 *Pinza*, was the first to arrive with nameplates attached and Nos D9001/3 received theirs at the same time. Haymarket and Gateshead 'Deltics' appeared in London during the summer, the former working the up 'Morning Talisman' ('Flying Scotsman' on Saturdays) and down 'Aberdonian' sleeper from 12 June, and the latter commencing a month later with the 7.56am from Newcastle, returning on the 4pm 'Talisman'.

Neville Hill also gained a duty to King's Cross from 12 June, using its new EE Type 4s Nos D345-8. They arrived on the overnight 10.50pm from Edinburgh, went to Leeds and back on the 'Queen of Scots' Pullman and then took out the 11.20pm Edinburgh train.

The first accelerated timing was introduced in the winter timetable, when the 'West Riding' had more than 30min pared from its schedule and was entrusted to Finsbury Park 'Deltics'. A second Gateshead 'Deltic' turn to London commenced, on the 'Tees-Tyne Pullman' and 5.35pm to Newcastle.

October 1961 saw the arrival of another prototype diesel, No D0280 *Falcon*, built by Brush. After two weeks of outings to Cambridge and Doncaster, *Falcon* went to Stratford and the Western Region for

The appearance of the prototype and production 'Deltics' make an interesting comparison. *Top:* ***Deltic*** takes the down 'White Rose' through Hadley Wood on 8 July 1959 and No D9009 ***Alycidon*** *Above:* — only four days after being delivered to Finsbury Park — heads the 10.25am from Newcastle between Hitchin and Stevenage on 5 August 1961. ***Alycidon's*** train consists almost entirely of LMS Stanier stock. *BR, Eastern Region; M. Pope*

trials, but it returned in April 1962 to take over the Sheffield Pullman workings, and remained until September. These trains had undergone a change of motive power in October 1961 when Sheffield Darnall Brush Type 2s replaced Finsbury Park EE Type 4s. Early in December 1961 three of the Type 2s uprated to 1,600bhp, Nos D5655-7, were transferred to Darnall and became regular performers on these duties.

A new outline was seen at King's Cross in the autumn of 1961 when on a number of occasions the 5.29pm from Leeds was brought in by a Neville Hill 'Peak'. Among them were No D29 on 4 November and No D25 11 days later.

One of the first long-distance inter-regional work-ings on BR began on 4 December with pairs of Southern Region BRCW Type 3s (Class 33) working through to York on the Cliffe-Uddingston cement

and return empties. Normally Hither Green based locomotives were used but on the last day of February 1962 'Hastings' gauge No D6590, based at St Leonards, was one of the pair.

The early months of 1962 saw Neville Hill's 'Peaks' continuing to arrive from time to time on the 5.29pm from Leeds and returning next morning on the 'White Rose', but an unusual occurrence was the use of Bristol Bath Road's No D35 on 9 January. In preparation for the allocation of 'Peaks' to the ECML, several of the later examples (which became Class 46) were on loan to ER depots early in 1962. Among them was No D154 which spent four months at Finsbury Park, but the others rarely ventured as far south as King's Cross. Delivery of Nos D166-93 to Gateshead began in May 1962 and their duties included the up 'Yorkshire Pullman', 'Tees-Tyne Pullman' and the fast 4.55pm from Newcastle.

Completion of the 'Deltics' in May was just in time for acceleration of ECML services the following month, in particular the introduction of 6hr timings for the 'Elizabethan', 'Flying Scotsman' and 'Talisman'. Earlier in the year one was seen on a freight, No D9019 taking the afternoon 'Scotch goods' on 10 March.

Probably the first sight of an English Electric Type 3 (Class 37) occurred on 29 April when GE Cambridge line trains were diverted via the ECML and Hitchin. On 17 June one was seen at Kings

Cross itself, Stratford's No D6729 taking the 2.40pm relief to Newcastle. Following the delivery of Nos D6742-54 to Darnall at that time, the Type 3 soon became part of the daily scene. The 7.20am (SO) from Sheffield was worked by No D6743 instead of *Falcon* on 4 August and a month later Type 3s took over the Sheffield Pullman duties. When Darnall became responsible for the Cleethorpes-King's Cross service on 5 November, however, Brush Type 2s were employed, although Type 3s appeared occasionally and assumed command in July 1963, by which time the depot also had Nos D6796-D6814.

Top left:
English Electric Type 1 No D8026 has Gateshead 'A1' No 60143 *Sir Walter Scott* for company at Hitchin shed on 7 March 1960. Pacifics were not infrequent visitors to the depot, often after failing in the area.
Michael Joyce
Left:
Soon after the type arrived at Finsbury Park depot, Paxman Type 1 No D8238 heads a lightweight Class 'K' freight at Crouch End on the Edgware branch in January 1961. *D. I. D. Loveday*
Below:
BR/Sulzer Type 2 No D5052 approaches Finsbury Park with an up freight in October 1961. *B. Haresnape*

An unusual visitor on 6 February 1963 was Crewe North EE Type 4 No D300, diverted to King's Cross with the up 'Royal Scot' due to blockage of the West Coast main line by snow. Other workings of note were the use of 'Deltic' No D9013 on the 6.30pm parcels to York on 21 May and EE Type 3 No D6735 of Hull Dairycoates on Roadrailer trials early in June.

The most significant event of 1963, however, was the build up of Brush Type 4s at Finsbury Park. The first, No D1500, had arrived at the end of September 1962, but delivery did not begin in earnest until the New Year. These locomotives were the main factor in bringing about the end of regular steam working the following summer. The early months of 1963 saw them employed on both main line freight and passenger turns including, from 1 April, the new '7-star' heavy freight hauls between Ferme Park and New England. By mid-June, more than 20 were on Finsbury Park's books. The diesels had arrived, and the stage was set for the elimination of steam from King's Cross.

Above:
Probably the first EE Type 3 to work through the King's Cross area, No D6701 comes off the Hertford Loop at Langley Junction with the diverted 2.36pm Liverpool Street-King's Lynn on 29 April 1962. Almost all the coaches stabled in the sidings are of Gresley design.
David Percival

Above:
A pair of Southern Region BRCW Type 3s, led by No D6571, roll the Uddingston-Cliffe cement empties towards Potters Bar in the summer of 1962. *P. J. Sharpe*

Below:
The ECML 'Peaks' were delivered to Gateshead in the latter part of 1962 and one of their regular duties was the up 'Yorkshire Pullman'. No D171 approaches Knebworth with the train on 14 January 1963. New Pullman Cars were introduced on this service two years earlier. *David Percival*

2

Great Northern Suburban

The year 1958 was the last in which steam loco-motives were in command of suburban services in the King's Cross area. The first diesel locomotive appeared in May of that year, when new Type 4 No D201 made several crew-training trips on scheduled trains between King's Cross and Cam-bridge. Other members of the class also worked Cambridge trains before progressing to main line work during the summer.

The basic off-peak service from King's Cross was an all-stations train at 30min past the hour to Hert-ford and one at 54min past to Hatfield, with an outer suburban departure at 21min past, calling at Hatfield and all stations to Baldock, Royston or Cambridge. Up services also ran to an hourly pattern and there were four 'Cambridge Buffet Express' services in each direction, calling at Welwyn Garden City, Hitchin and Letchworth and, sometimes, Baldock or Royston. Standard journey times were 57min to Hertford, just over 50min to Hatfield and just under an hour-and-a-half to Baldock. Cambridge stopping trains completed the journey in 2hr.

Steam timings were retained during the winter of 1958 and the early months of 1959, as Cravens diesel units and Type 2 locomotives gradually entered service, and the first revision of schedules came with the summer 1959 timetable. To Hertford there were DMU trains at three and 30min past the hour, the latter an 'all-stations' on a 51min timing. The inner suburban service on the main line was extended to Welwyn Garden City, with a departure at 40min past the hour calling at Finsbury Park, Oakleigh Park and all stations to the garden city, reached in 46min. A new 'all-stations' ran from Finsbury Park to Hatfield, connecting with the Hert-ford train leaving the 'Cross' at 3min past the hour.

Below:
The Great Northern atmosphere is still present on 24 July 1958 when the 7.22am King's Cross-Hertford North, headed by 'N2' No 69574, emerges from Copenhagen Tunnel and climbs Holloway Bank.
Brian Morrison

Outer suburban departures were moved to the half-hour and accelerated by 15min to Baldock. The New Town of Stevenage gained the service of the 'Cambridge Buffet Express' trains.

As an experiment, the 'Buffet' sets were utilised on two new return services to Royston, one a late morning/early afternoon working and the other as the 5.26pm departure from King's Cross, returning at 8.04pm. The buffet cars were open on all these trains and were particularly well patronised by homeward-bound commuters on the 5.26! In the

following September the Royston trains were extended to Cambridge. A year later, the 3.05pm down 'Buffet' was extended from Cambridge to Ely, in place of a previous DMU service, and returned at 5.33pm. This arrangement lasted until April 1966.

After 1959, steam locomotives continued on some workings until the last two — both diagrammed for Cambridge 4-6-0s — were taken over by Brush Type 2 diesels in October 1960. This virtually ended the reign of the steam locomotive on King's Cross suburban services, although some of the Peter-

Top:
In the early days of dieselisation, on 19 March 1959, a four-car Cravens unit enters the 'Cross' as the 1.10pm from Baldock. A North British Type 2 and an English Electric Type 4 await their next duties in the locomotive sidings. The spotters on Platform 10 are more interested in the arrival of 'A4' No 60013 *Dominion of New Zealand* with an express! *Michael Joyce*

Above:
Three Class 312 diagrams were introduced on 3 October 1977. On that morning, Nos 312 003 and 312 005 were the rear units of, respectively, the 07.13 from Royston and 08.01 from Stevenage. The headcodes and destinations have already been set up for their return workings on the 17.46 to Hitchin and the 17.42 to Royston. *David Percival*

borough stopping trains remained steam-powered until June 1963.

An interesting working on which Hitchin's 'J15' No 65479 ended its days was the unadvertised Saturday morning RAF leave train from Henlow Camp — the limit of ER responsibility on the LMR Bedford branch. On arrival at Hitchin the train changed engines and became a public service to Broad Street (Kings Cross from November 1959). In 1959/60 the train might be worked forward by either a steam or diesel locomotive — and the same happened on those occasions when one of Hitchin's 204bhp diesels was standing in for the veteran 0-6-0!

Passenger services on the branch ended at the beginning of 1962 but, a few miles further south, a regular 'branch' passenger service was soon to be operating again for the first time since 1939. In March 1962 a modest service was introduced in the morning and evening 'peaks' between Hertford North and Stevenage, some trains also serving Hitchin. Three months later an hourly Saturday service was added. Intermediate stations at Stapleford and Watton-at-Stone remained closed, though the latter was re-opened 20 years later.

King's Cross suburban services were not entirely spared from the cutbacks of the 1960s, for the axe fell on the Dunstable branch in 1965. Since September 1962, Cravens diesel units had worked the line, but locomotive-hauled trains were employed to cope with the 'last day' traffic on 24 April. That day's

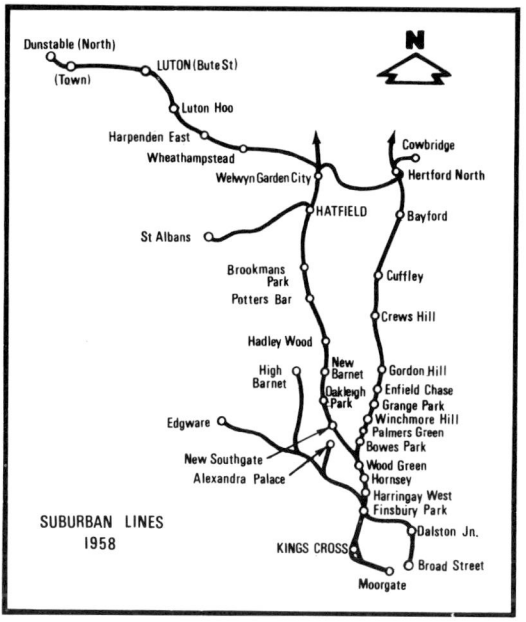

Below:
Re-opening day at Watton-at-Stone, 17 May 1982, sees modest business as '313' No 313 037 pauses on the 15.02 Letchworth–Moorgate working. 60% of the forecast traffic level had been reached within a year.
David Percival

15

6.18pm Dunstable-Hatfield was formed of a Quad Art set and hauled by EE Type 1 No D8046, its headboard proclaiming the fact that this was the 'Last Skimpot Flyer'.

The LNER buffet car in one of the two 'Cambridge Buffet Express' sets was replaced by a BR miniature buffet car (RMB) in September 1962 and the workings covered by that set lost their title in the June 1963 public timetable. Although the name was restored the following winter it lasted only another nine months, for the 'Cambridge Buffet Express' title was dropped from all the buffet workings in June 1964. Nevertheless, patrons continued to use the old title until the trains were withdrawn in February 1978 when the Royston electric service commenced.

In the late-1960s, the hourly Finsbury Park-Hatfield service was extended to form an additional train from King's Cross, calling at all stations to Welwyn Garden City. At the same time, the outer suburban departure was moved to 5min past the hour, and this pattern remained until the end of the diesel period.

The electric era began with reinstatement of the former London Transport Northern City service, which had ended in October 1975 when BR took over the line. From 16 August 1976, Class 313 units

Suburban steam on the branches.
Above: **Diverted via the Hertford Loop due to engineering work on Sunday 31 August 1958, 'B17' No 61652** *Darlington* **approaches Stapleford with the 1.56pm from Cambridge.** *Right:* **'N7' No 69618 heads the 6.25pm Dunstable-Hatfield away from Luton Hoo on 10 July 1959. Great Northern somersault signals survived on the branch until closure.**
Both: J. F. Aylard

Top:
At Luton Bute Street on the last day of the branch passenger service, 24 April 1965, a Cravens DMU forms the 5.10pm Dunstable-Welwyn Garden City and Brush Type 2 No D5589 heads the 5.13pm Welwyn-Dunstable. The Midland main line is in the background.
David Percival

Above:
Cravens DMUs at Hertford North on the evening of 24 June 1976 stand beneath the 'overhead' which will power their replacements in little more than four months time. *David Percival*

operated a 10min interval service between Drayton Park and Old Street; work still in progress on escalators at Moorgate precluded through running to the City terminus.

The last Eastern Region suburban trains to and from Broad Street and Moorgate via the Widened Lines ran on the morning of Saturday 6 November 1976. On the following Monday, 8 November, the electric inner suburban service was launched, with a regular 20min interval pattern throughout the day between Moorgate and both Welwyn Garden City and Hertford North; previously there was a half-hourly service on both routes. During the morning and evening 'peaks', the frequency was increased to six Welwyn Garden City trains and nine on the Hertford line. An hourly all-night service was introduced, with a diesel train running between King's Cross and Wood Green, connecting there with an electric service to both Hertford and Welwyn Garden City. The diesel shuttle was withdrawn in October 1977 when these Welwyn Garden City trains were extended to King's Cross.

At weekends, a 20min service operated on Saturdays, while Sunday trains were increased from one an hour to one every half-hour on both lines. Standard timings of 40min from Moorgate to Welwyn and about the same to Hertford (depending upon intermediate stops) saved about 10min over the previous times from King's Cross.

As described in Chapter 11, some outer suburban electric trains were introduced on diesel timings in the autumn of 1977, and the full electric service commenced on 6 February 1978. Class 312 units operated an off-peak service of two trains an hour calling at Finsbury Park, Potters Bar, Hatfield and all stations to Royston, and a third making intermediate stops only at Stevenage, Hitchin and Letchworth. Stopping trains were timed at 62min (down) and 61min (up), while the fast trains' schedule was 50min (down) and 48min (up). The latter's generous allowance of 27 or 28min between King's Cross and Stevenage has enabled a Finsbury Park stop to be included (since June 1981) without affecting the overall timing. Otherwise, apart from alterations to departure times, the pattern of Monday-Saturday services has remained unchanged. On Sundays, however, the half-hourly service (there is no fast train) was reduced to one train an hour in October 1981.

With the introduction of outer suburban electrification, connecting DMU shuttle services commenced between Hertford (Hitchin on Sundays) and Huntingdon and between Royston and Cambridge, operated by refurbished Metro-Cammell (Class 101) DMUs. On Mondays-Saturdays since May 1979, however, one of the Moorgate-Hertford trains is extended to and from Letchworth every hour (also on Sundays since October 1981) and the Huntingdon service operates to and from Hitchin only.

An innovation from June 1981 was the running of three morning 'peak' services from Welwyn to King's Cross, and three evening trains in the reverse direc-

Above:
Through working between King's Cross and Cambridge ended on Sunday 5 February 1978. On that day, Class 31 No 31.404 passes Shepreth Junction with the 09.20 up 'buffet'. *John M. Capes*

Above:

Broad Street was the Saturday terminus for some suburban services whose Monday-Friday destination was King's Cross. Such was the case with the 6.55am from Cambridge and the 8.23am from Hatfield, approaching New Barnet on 11 March 1961 hauled by Brush Type 2s Nos D5608 and D5601, respectively. The four-character headcodes, with their third digit indicating 'Broad Street', were introduced two months earlier. *J. F. Aylard*

Below:

Electric unit No 313 010 waits to depart from Moorgate as the 14.50 service to Welwyn Garden City on 15 January 1977. *Brian Morrison*

tion. These were reduced to one each way in October 1982. The same autumn timetable revision switched the Sunday Moorgate-Hertford-Letchworth service to King's Cross and these trains now provide the Hertford line with its only regular Class 312 workings.

A brief reference was made earlier in this chapter to the Peterborough stopping trains. During the 1960s and 1970s considerable changes were made, although a handful of through trains continue to the present time in the morning and evening 'peaks'. In the 1970s an irregular service was operating between Hitchin and Peterborough, connecting with

the outer suburban service at Hitchin. The Royston electric service has provided Huntingdon and intermediate stations north of Hitchin with an hourly service to London, though there are few opportunities to connect with ECML trains at Peterborough.

During the 1970s, modernisation affected almost every station in the area, notably King's Cross itself with its new concourse in June 1973, and the provision of a new station one mile south of the original at Stevenage, opened on 23 July 1973. Track realignment left Harringay and Hornsey with platforms on the slow lines only, and the quadrupling through Sandy and Huntingdon (in the mid-1970s) resulted in virtually new stations. During the rebuilding, many Great Northern structures were demolished, but some of those which remain have been thoughtfully incorporated into the modern railway scene.

The stations at Three Counties, Arlesey and Henlow, and Offord and Buckden closed to passenger traffic early in 1959, and those on the Dunstable branch in April 1965. But recent years have seen a station re-opened. On 17 May 1982 — on which day Wood Green station was renamed Alexandra Palace — Watton-at-Stone station, between Hertford North and Stevenage, welcomed regular passenger trains for the first time in nearly 43 years.

Below:
'A3' No 60061 *Pretty Polly*, fitted with small smoke deflectors, pauses at Hatfield, its first stop from the 'Cross', with the 7.21pm to Peterborough in the summer of 1961. Top Shed's Pacifics regularly headed the train, which was formed of non-corridor stock at this period. Brush Type 2 No D5647 stands alongside. *Jeff Topple*

Bottom:
In 1983, until becoming an HST duty in October, the 07.00 from Peterborough normally sported a pair of Class 31s or a '47', but Class 37s appeared from time to time — No 37.090 on several occasions. On 10 March it is unusually paired with No 31.264, and seems a little out of sorts departing from Stevenage! *David Percival*

3
Main Line Passenger Service

'King's Cross for Scotland' ran the publicity slogan of the late 1950s. True — but also for the north-east, and the West Riding, plus destinations in what are now North and South Humberside, Sheffield and even a service from Nottingham (a through train at 7.33am via Grantham to King's Cross).

The fastest timings to Edinburgh in 1958 were around 6¾hr, while to Leeds the best was the non-stop 'Queen of Scots' Pullman, taking just under 3½hr. No less than 15 titled expresses were running in the 1958 summer timetable, including the seasonal 'Elizabethan', 'Norseman' and 'Scarborough Flyer', plus the short-lived 'Fair Maid'. The last-mentioned — along with the 'Heart of Midlothian' — were Edinburgh trains extended to Perth in the autumn of 1957, but both returned to their previous schedules in September 1958 and the 'Fair Maid' reverted to its 'Morning Talisman' title.

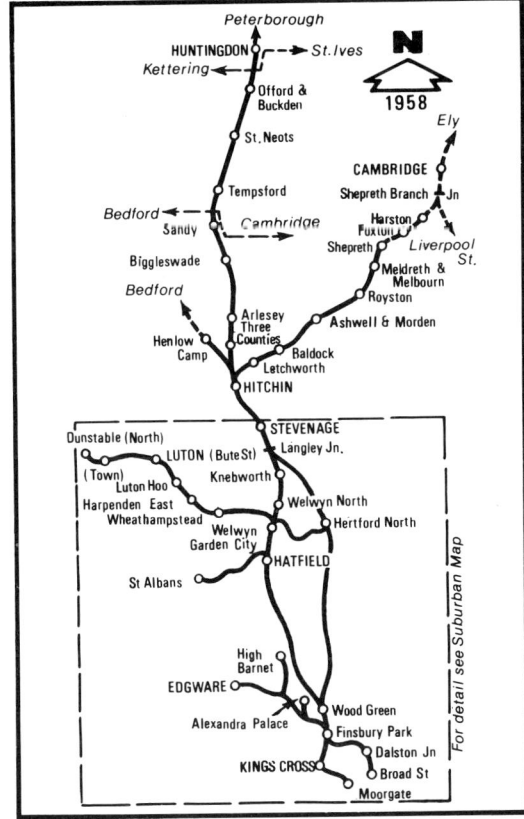

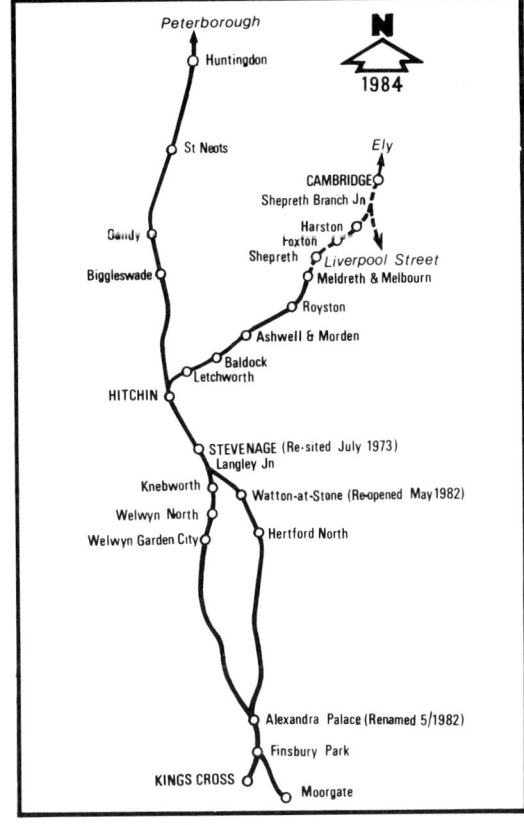

Below:
Just on 2 o'clock and no more passengers are hurrying for the Newcastle train on Platform 8, which had arrived as the 8am from Newcastle behind 'A1' No 60151 *Midlothian* on 16 September 1958. 'A1' No 60119 *Patrick Stirling* had brought in the 9.15am from York and its train is returning in 10min time. Almost the full depth of the concourse is visible in this photograph.
Michael Joyce

Bottom:
Gateshead 'A3' No 60040 *Cameronian* finds itself on a Top Shed Pacific diagram, leaving King's Cross with the 7.50am 'Fair Maid' on 17 July 1958. The extension of this morning Anglo-Scottish train to Perth lasted only from September 1957 until September 1958.
R. F. Orpwood

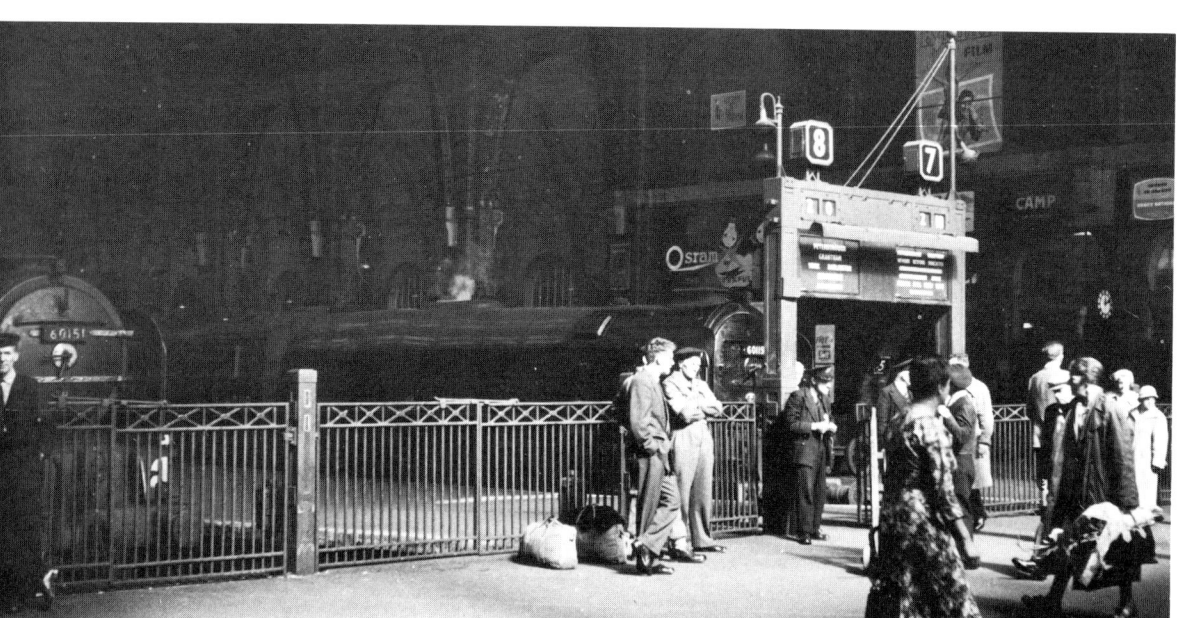

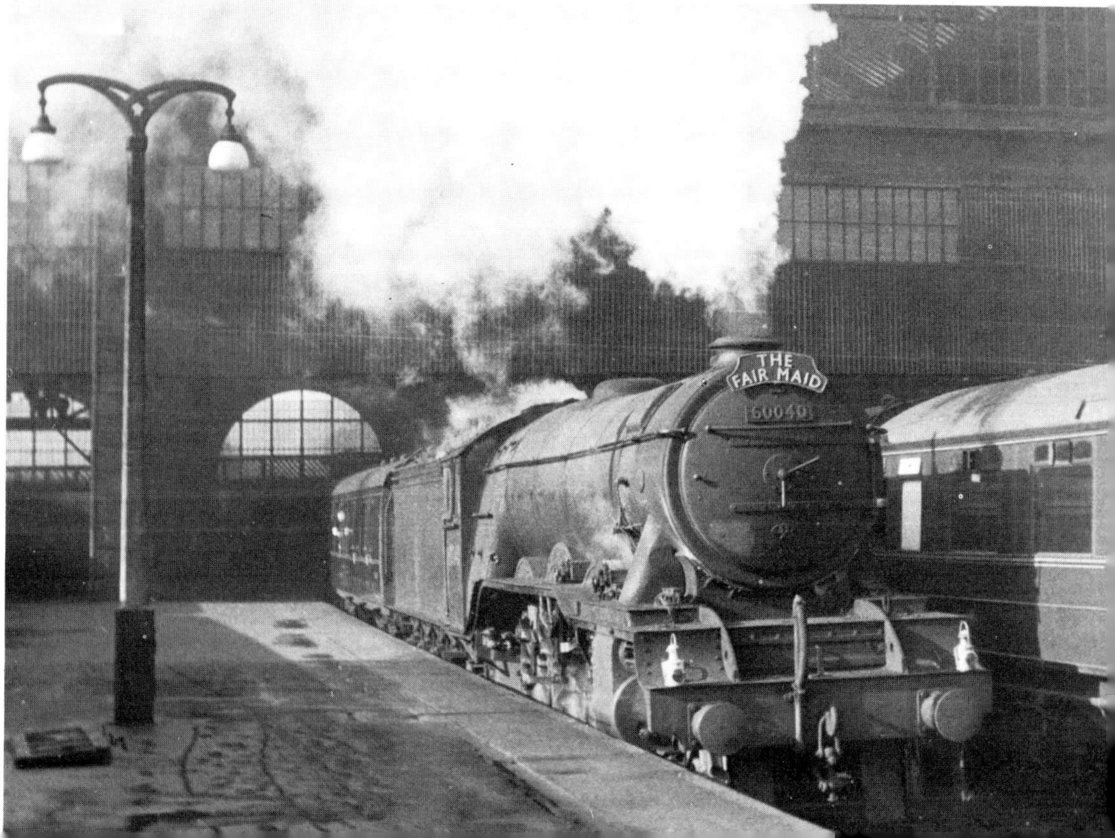

Above:
**'Deltic' No 9003 *Meld* heads the up 'Tees-Tyne
Pullman', with its mixture of Pullman and ordinary stock
at Wymondley, between Hitchin and Stevenage in
1971.** *D. J. Rice*

Perth was also served by an overnight car-carrying train, the 'Car Sleeper Limited'; a daytime equivalent, the 'Anglo-Scottish Car Carrier' (to Edinburgh), was launched in the summer of 1960. At the same time, car-loading facilities in King's Cross Goods Yard were replaced by a new terminal at Holloway, which was used by these trains until a new London 'Motorail' terminal was completed at Kensington Olympia in 1967.

New services introduced in the late-1950s were the Sheffield Pullmans (the morning up and evening down trains titled 'Master Cutler') in September 1958, and the 'Tees-Thames' — a through service between Saltburn and King's Cross — in November 1959. The latter ran until the autumn of 1961, when Saltburn was better served by connections with the newly-accelerated north-east trains. In September 1959 the 'West Riding' title was transferred in the down direction from the 3.40pm to a morning departure and, 'Queen of Scots' excepted, became the fastest service to and from Leeds. This express was the first to benefit from 'Deltic' haulage two years later, with more than half an hour cut from its schedule on 11 September 1961, giving the down train a 3hr 9min timing and the up an even 3hr. At the same time, the already fast 7.50am from Newcastle was accelerated by no less than 50min.

Even more impressive were the June 1962 improvements. The stars were the three 6hr Edinburgh trains — the 'Flying Scotsman', 'Talisman' and 'Elizabethan' (which lost the non-stop status it enjoyed when 'A4s' were in command). A total of 15 down and 11 up trains on Mondays to Fridays were accelerated and designated for 'Deltic' haulage.

One effect of the shorter journey times between the two Capitals was to lessen the appeal of the 'Queen of Scots'; its route via Leeds gave an overall timing of $7\frac{1}{2}$hr between London and Edinburgh. From June 1964 it was discontinued north of Leeds and renamed the 'White Rose', taking the title of an existing express. Only one rake of Pullmans was now required for the service and some of the surplus cars were redeployed as first class accommodation in one of the sets operating on the 'Talisman' which, for a few months, ran as a part-Pullman train — a concept later applied to all ECML Pullmans.

Late 1965 saw the end of King's Cross-Glasgow through services, apart from the Fort William

23

2 | The journey shrinker | 1

HIGH SPEED TRAINS Passenger Accommodation

HIGH SPEED TRAINS Catering Facilities

254 014

Above:
Cleaning of the station roof is under way as HST No 254 014 stands at the 'Cross' on 20 June 1978 during the first 'InterCity 125' timetable. The effect of the banner is somewhat marred by miscellaneous notices leaning against the barrier! *Brian Loudwell*

portion of some overnight trains; through trains to Glasgow have been reinstated in recent years. In that same autumn the Sheffield Pullmans were re-routed from the city's Victoria to the Midland station.

Major changes came with the timetable commencing on 18 April 1966, notably a fast Leeds service at 07.25 up and 15.55 down, 'Deltic'-hauled and running to a non-stop timing of 160 minutes at an average speed of 70mph. A Bradford service (07.36 up and 15.20 down) calling only at Wakefield was almost as fast, even though the 15.20 was booked for a Type 4 locomotive. As a result, the 'West Riding' name was dropped from the now less prestigious morning trains. North-east and Scottish services were revised, with 'even hour' Edinburgh and 'odd hour' Newcastle departures between 08.00 and 18.00. Similar adjustments to the up services gave Newcastle 11 trains each way at equal intervals. Leeds trains were retimed to depart from King's Cross at 25min past the 'odd' hours, while departures at 20min past the 'even' hours served Doncaster, York and Hull, including some additional trains to Leeds and Newcastle.

Further revision of Pullman Car services occurred in the late 1960s. The 'White Rose' was replaced by a new, fast, Leeds service in March 1967 and the spare cars formed a separate 'Hull Pullman' (previously the 'Yorkshire Pullman' had included a Hull portion). On 4 October 1968 the Sheffield Pullmans made their last journeys and the 'Master Cutler' name (but not the stock) was transferred to the St Pancras route. On the following Monday the second class cars of the 'Hull Pullman' were replaced by ordinary stock and catering cars; similar changes were effected on the 'Tees-Tyne' in May 1969 and the 'Yorkshire Pullman' in May 1971.

A bold experiment began on 4 May 1970 when a cheap fare service was introduced between Finsbury Park and Newcastle, calling at Potters Bar and Stevenage and running via Stockton and Sunderland. The 'Highwayman', as the train was titled, completed its journey in just under 6hr, compared with around 4½hr for most Newcastle services and just over 3½hr for the fastest of them, accelerated on the same day. But the attraction to impecunious travellers (whom BR aimed to entice from road coach services) was the single fare of 35 shillings (£1.75); the normal single fare was 86 shillings (£4.30). For the railway enthusiast, the leisurely pace, unusual routing and LNER buffet cars provided further interest. In contrast, the two years during which the train operated saw a determined drive to attract business travel. Up trains from Leeds, Bradford and Newcastle due in

Above:
**Class 47 No 47.401 *North Eastern* heads the up
'Nightrider' at Wymondley on 19 June 1983. The way
the train leans shows how the curve has been adapted
for 125mph running** *David Percival*

London between 10.00 and 11.00, together with return services at 15.55, 16.05 and 18.00 respectively, gained the title 'Executive', although the names did not appear in the public timetables until 1974.

Departures from the scene in May 1976 were another Pullman, the 'Tees-Tyne', and the restaurant car (operating to York) on the rear of the early evening Aberdeen sleeper, then leaving the 'Cross' at 20.00. Aberdonians accustomed to dining before turning in could travel on the new 19.50 restaurant car train to York and join the 20.00 there, but one wonders if many did!

To commemorate Her Majesty's Silver Jubilee, a famous East Coast title was revived for the 07.45 King's Cross-Edinburgh and 15.00 return during the summer of 1977. On the first day, 8 June, Class 55 No 55.012 was immaculately turned out for the down train and it was pleasing to see that a headboard had been provided. The 'Silver Jubilee' motif was printed on carriage window labels and on a window blind of the buffet car, in which photographs of the prewar streamliner were displayed. By the end of the month, however, use of the headboard was less than meticulous and the turnout of the 'Deltics' (and even '47s') was less than immaculate. Timekeeping of the up train began to slip and it was perhaps a blessing that the title was withdrawn after a few months.

Introduction of the first HST timetable in May 1978 resulted in acceleration of the fastest Edinburgh

trains by some 30-60min, with 20-50min cuts in the timings of Newcastle trains. Additional locomotive-hauled trains were the so-called 'sweeper' services, calling at most intermediate ECML stations and connecting at York with the HSTs. Many were hauled by the displaced 'Deltics'. The last of the non-standard daytime formations had been the 'Hull Pullman' and 'Yorkshire Pullman', which made their final runs on 5 May.

Despite the exhilarating influence of the High Speed Trains, the early months of 1979 were unhappy times for all concerned with East Coast main line services. In January came a series of ASLEF 24hr strikes, which, even on 'normal' days, effectively halted overnight services. Then, at the end of the month, several trains were withdrawn due to shortage of stock. This situation lasted for some weeks, at the end of which the planners' hopes for the 1979 timetable were dashed by the collapse of Penmanshiel Tunnel, blocking the line between Berwick and Edinburgh for five months. The timetable had to be redrafted, with most ECML services running to and from Berwick and others (including the overnights) diverted via Carlisle.

Three phases of the 'Flying Scotsman'. *Above:*
York-based 'A2/2' No 60502 *Earl Marischal* recalls an
earlier period when New England locomotives of this
type took the train out of King's Cross. It is approaching
Hitchin on 31 July 1959, standing in for a Gateshead
Pacific which normally worked the down 'Scotsman'
during that summer. *Above right:* **The first '6-hr'
northbound 'Scotsman' approaches Harringay on
18 June 1962 behind immaculately-groomed 'Deltic' No
D9020 *Nimbus*. *Right:* On 28 March 1964, 'Deltic'
No D9016 (still to be named) carries the winged-thistle
headboard introduced earlier that month as it lifts the
down train past Finsbury Park.**
Michael Joyce; D. I. D. Loveday; David Percival

The one bright spot of the year was the acceleration of the 'Deltic'-hauled 'Hull Executive' in May.
Until retired a year later, the down train, at 17.05,
was allowed 91min for the 138 miles to Retford. Its
average speed of 91.3mph is still the record for a
British locomotive-hauled train, West Coast electrics
included.

An unofficial, though appropriate, title was carried
by the 17.12 to Grantham on Friday 9 May 1980.
From the following Monday the train was to run as
far as Peterborough only and '47' No 47.418 which
worked the train on that Friday was adorned with a
'Grantham Executive' headboard. A further official
'Executive' name appeared when a through HST
service to and from the north-east coast was

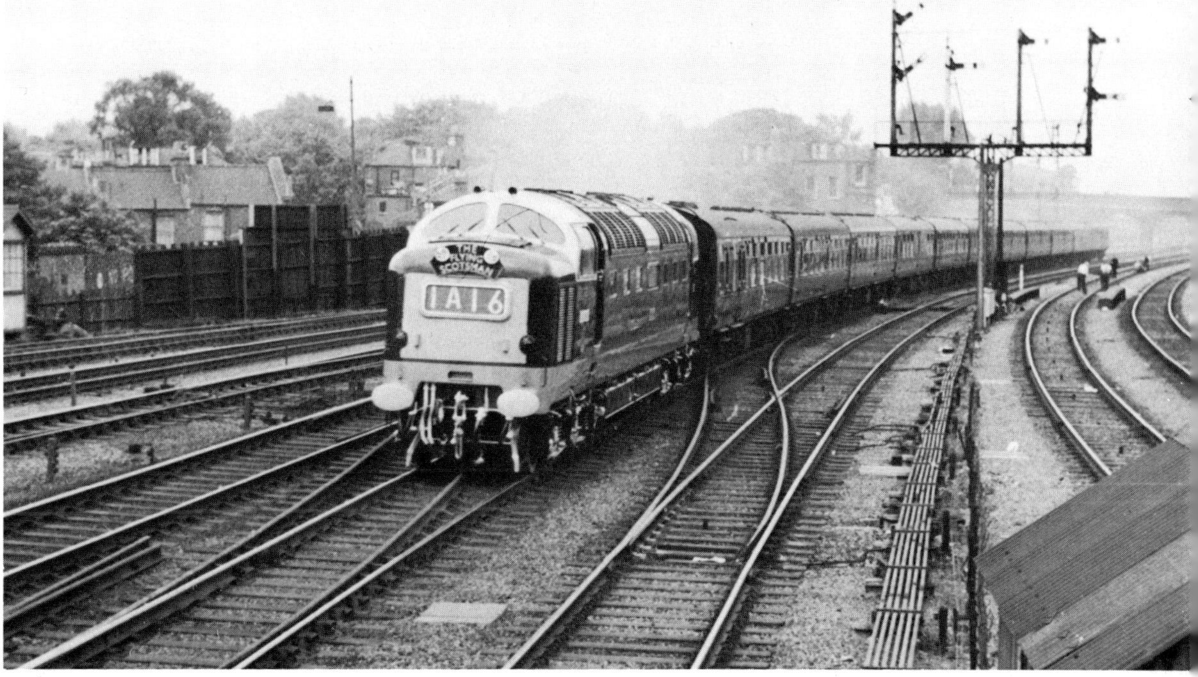
1A16

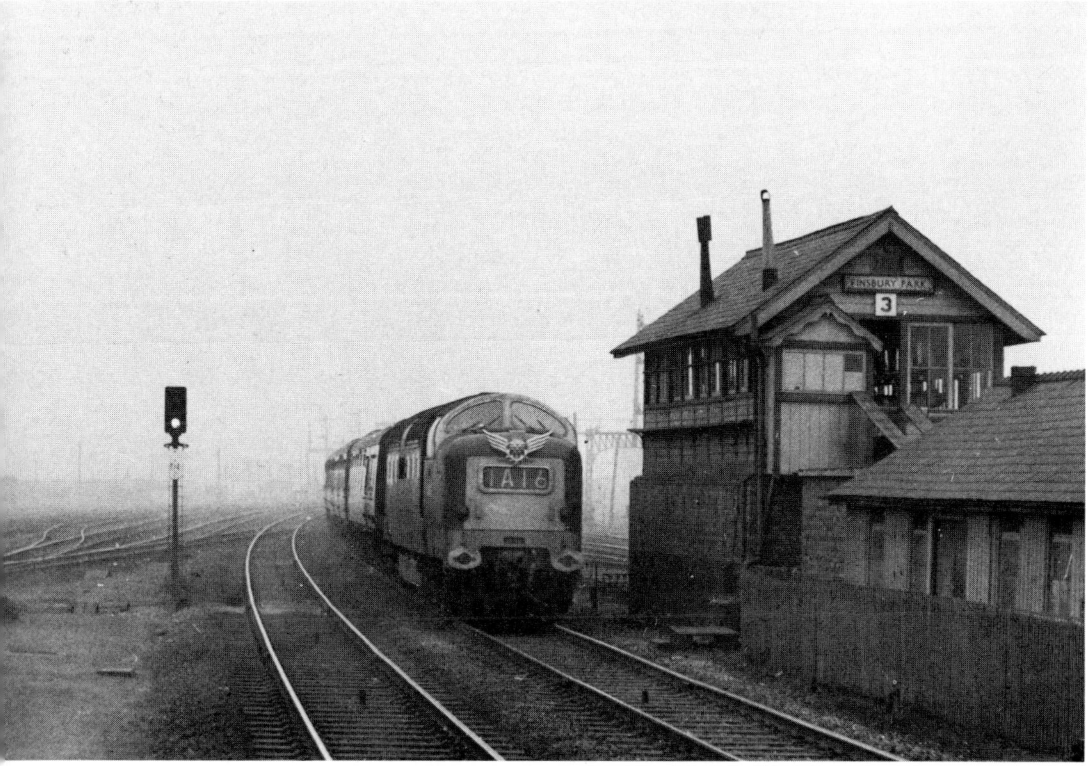
FINSBURY PARK
3
1A16

introduced in January 1981. The 07.10 from Middlesbrough and 16.40 return were entitled 'Cleveland Executive'; un-named services, at 07.25 down and 16.40 up, were added in June 1981. At this date it was possible to reach virtually every ECML destination direct from Stevenage, via the early morning series of expresses which called there. From King's Cross these were the 05.50 to Aberdeen, 07.10 to Newcastle, 07.25 to Middlesbrough, 07.45 to Bradford, 08.00 to Edinburgh, 08.05 to Hull, 08.30 to Cleethorpes and 08.50 to Harrogate. All but the 05.50 and 08.30 were HST services. Within two years, however, the early morning service had been reduced to the 05.45 to York, 07.30 to Newcastle, 07.50 to Leeds, 08.00 to Edinburgh and 08.04 to Hull (all calling at Stevenage) and 08.50 to Leeds.

Below:
Traditional cars, single-chimney 'A3' and semaphore signals combine nostalgically as No 60039 *Sandwich* heads the down 'Yorkshire Pullman' between the tunnels at Welwyn on 11 July 1958.
E. R. Wethersett/Ian Allan Library

During those two years, the 'Flying Scotsman' underwent some significant changes. From June 1981 it commenced its southbound journey at 07.20 from Aberdeen, but the down train broke further from tradition a year later, when the 10.00 departure was extended to Aberdeen and took the 'Aberdonian' title from the 12.00 service. The removal of the 'Scotsman' from its time-honoured spot to 10.35 was the subject of a letter to *The Times*! Nevertheless, the 'Scotsman' retained its prestige as the fastest service to and from Edinburgh, with new timings of 4hr 35min (down) and 4hr 38min southbound. Its 10.00 departure from King's Cross was restored in May 1984, with both up and down trains serving Aberdeen and accelerated to exactly 4½hr between King's Cross and Edinburgh.

Alterations to overnight services resulted from the introduction of Mk III sleeping cars in 1982. A new Aberdeen train at 21.00 (21.08 on Saturdays) commenced on 17 May, formed of Mk IId open seconds and the new sleepers. It became an all-sleeper service on 7 June, the 20.00 lost its Mk I sleeping cars from

Top:
'B1' No 61179 — a favourite on these trains in 1962 — gets under way with a 'Butlin's Express' for Skegness on 9 June 1962. *R. F. Orpwood*

Above:
'Deltic' No 55.007 *Pinza* leaves Stevenage with the second northbound 'Silver Jubilee' on 9 June 1977. *David Percival*

the same date and was discontinued in May 1983. In October 1983 the 21.00 was retimed to depart at 20.25.

A new low-fare overnight service, the 'Nightrider', began in May 1982, with single fares of £12 to Edinburgh (where the train divided) and Glasgow, £14 to Dundee and £16 to Aberdeen. Passengers enjoyed travel in Mk IId open firsts, with subdued blue lighting which earned the train the nickname the 'blue lagoon'. An all night buffet service was provided. Since May 1983, when a similar service was introduced between Euston and Glasgow, the complete train has run through to Aberdeen.

Re-casting of the ECML service from May 1984 has followed the opening of the Selby diversion the previous autumn. Among the new timetable's features are a through service to and from Inverness (Perth during the winter months), departing northbound at 12.00, and operation of the semi-fast 'sweepers' between King's Cross and Doncaster (instead of York or Hull) except for some morning and evening business services.

Above:
With Class 40 No 254 in charge on 16 May 1970, the down 'Highwayman' arrives at the original Stevenage station (replaced three years later). The fifth coach of the train is an ex-LNER Thompson buffet car.
David Percival

Below:
One of the 'sweeper' services introduced that summer, the Sunday 12.05 York-King's Cross arrives at Huntingdon on 10 September 1978, hauled by No 47.525. The last locomotive-hauled York 'semi-fasts' were replaced by HSTs in May 1982.
John C. Baker

4

The End of Steam

Until the arrival of the main line diesels in the late 1950s, steam locomotives handled all passenger and freight services within and running into the King's Cross area. Most were relatively modern and, except those used on heavy freights, of LNER design. At the beginning of 1958, the up-to-date steam locomotive was especially prominent on outer suburban passenger services where the lion's share of the work was handled by postwar Thompson 'B1' 4-6-0s and 'L1' 2-6-4Ts based at King's Cross and Hitchin. A trio of BR Standard '5' 4-6-0s, Nos 73157-9, was allocated to King's Cross, and Cambridge shed contributed 4-6-0s of Classes 'B1', 'B2' and 'B17'.

Peppercorn 'A1' Pacifics, built in 1948/9, were proving masters of main line express work, although 'A4s' continued to power the prestige trains and the older 'A3s' were favourites at some sheds. Less

Below:
At the end of 1959, 'B1s' Nos 61026 and 61248 joined No 61379 *Mayflower* **to make a trio of named examples among Immingham's 'B1' fleet (though No 61026** *Ourebi* **remained only for three months). On the arduous Cleethorpes working, No 61248** *Geoffrey Gibbs* **has completed nearly 130 miles of its journey as it passes beneath 'penny ha'penny' footbridge at Wymondley.**
D. Ludford

important express passenger services were also entrusted to 'A2s' and 'V2' 2-6-2s. Immingham's two daily return workings from Cleethorpes were probably the most demanding of all 'B1' duties. Two unique locomotives based at Doncaster, the 'A1/1' rebuild No 60113 *Great Northern* and the 'W1' 4-6-4 No 60700, were both seen regularly at the 'Cross'.

Fitted freights were mostly in the hands of 'V2' 2-6-2s, 'K3' 2-6-0s and 'B1s', but new '9F' 2-10-0s allocated to Doncaster were appearing in London on express freights. Power for the heavy coal trains running up the main line to Ferme Park was provided by New England's '9Fs' and wartime 'WD' 2-8-0s.

Only in the inner suburban area was there a distinctive pre-1923 Great Northern flavour. Class 'N2' 0-6-2Ts handled the bulk of passenger services and empty stock workings, while shunting and freight duties occupied 'J50' 0-6-0Ts and the few remaining 'J52' 0-6-0STs. Examples of another GNR class, the

Contrasting scenes at three of the area's steam depots.

Above: Visible from the down platform at Hitchin on 1 August 1958 are 'B1s' Nos 61093 and 61391, 'L1' No 67744 — the last steam locomotive allocated when the steam depot closed in November 1960 — and 'J15' No 65479. *Below:* An enthusiasts' visit to Hornsey in the summer of 1961 finds many of the depot's 'N2', 'J50' and 'J94' tank engines out of use. 'J50' No 68950 and 'J94' No 68073 are at the near end of this line. *Bottom:* Less than five months before closure, the line-up at 'Top Shed' on 27 January 1963 shows 'WD' No 90151; 'A3s' Nos 60061 *Pretty Polly*, 60053 *Sansovino* and 60047 *Donovan*; 'A4' No 60007 *Sir Nigel Gresley*; and 'B1' No 61394.

Michael Joyce; D. Ludford; David Percival

The 'BR Standard' look. *Above:* **Class '5' No 73157 approaches Brookmans Park with the 2.16pm down 'Cambridge Buffet Express' on 18 June 1958.** *Above right:* **One of New England's numerous '9Fs', No 92181, heads a down Class 'E' freight on the Hertford Loop north of Cuffley on 23 October 1958.** *Right:* **'Britannia' No 70039 *Sir Christopher Wren*, one of the first to be allocated to Immingham, leaves King's Cross with the 4.10pm to Cleethorpes on 26 April 1961.** *C. T. Gifford; BR, Eastern Region; G. A. Richardson*

'J6' 0-6-0, were based at Hornsey and Hitchin for light freight duties.

A Great Eastern presence was evident at Hitchin, the home of three 'J68' 0-6-0Ts and a solitary 'J15' 0-6-0, and at Hatfield, which housed a number of 'N7' 0-6-2Ts for Dunstable branch trains. Steam in the area included a variety of Bedford-based locomotives working to Hitchin over the LMR branch. Further south, locomotives from other regions appeared on cross-London freight trips to Ferme Park yards.

Occasional visitors included 'B16' 4-6-0s from York, 'O2' and 'O4' 2-8-0s from the Doncaster and Lincolnshire areas, 'O1' 2-8-0s from March, 'B12' 4-6-0s, 'K1' 2-6-0s and various 0-6-0s from Great Eastern section sheds, and the odd 'Britannia' — particularly after overhaul of these Pacifics was transferred to Doncaster Works in mid-1958.

Such was the motive power scene only five years before steam was officially banned south of Hitchin.

But those five years were to see developments which enabled steam power to perform a valuable role during the period of transition. Not the least of their tasks was the requirement for Pacifics to substitute effectively for Type 4 diesels on express passenger services. The fitting of double-chimneys to the 'A4s' — completed in 1958 — and to the 'A3s' during 1958/9 assisted King's Cross and Gateshead in maintaining schedules and turn-round times that were designed for diesels. From early 1958, new '9Fs' No 92178 and No 92183 onwards were built with double chimneys. The last of the Eastern Region series, No 92202, was delivered to Immingham in February 1959 and joined by others transferred from New England and Doncaster. They took over the daily fish train working to London, previously the province of 'K3s', and in Immingham fashion were smartly turned out and embellished with silver painted smokebox door hinges and straps. The deficiency in heavy freight power at New England was made up with more 'WDs' which as a result increasingly appeared on the Peterborough-London freights.

Double chimneys were fitted to a handful of 'V2s' in 1960/1. Towards the end of the steam period, three of them, Nos 60817/80/1, were based at New England as main line pilots and frequently brought expresses to King's Cross following a diesel locomotive failure.

In December 1958, 'J94' 0-6-0ST No 68033 was transferred to Hornsey; it was joined by Nos 68067/73/5/7 early in 1959, and the last duties of the 'J52s' were taken over by the newcomers. A second 'new' class of locomotive to appear regularly was the 'Britannia', three of which were moved to Immingham late in 1960. Within a year, Nos 70035-41 were based there and had ousted 'B1s' from the two newly-accelerated daily passenger turns from Cleethorpes.

For brief periods, three more types — all tank engines — put in an appearance. Class 'A5' 4-6-2Ts Nos 69824 and 69814 were on loan to Top Shed in February 1958 and for the first six months of 1960, respectively, mainly for working ECS trains. In September 1958, BR Standard '4' 2-6-4Ts Nos 80103/37 were loaned by Neasden and joined King's Cross 'L1s' on outer suburban services for a couple of weeks. Hatfield shed gained 'N5' No 69266 for two months from the end of July 1959; the 0-6-2T was used on the Welwyn Garden City-Hertford branch.

The run down of steam power affected first the suburban passenger locomotives. Among the classes rapidly depleted were the 'N2s' and 'N7s', while Cambridge's 'B2s' and 'B17s' were all withdrawn or transferred away by the end of 1959. Class 'B17s' continued to reach the 'Cross' when Cambridge borrowed them for its remaining steam duties, which continued until October 1960. The last flurry of visits by 'B12s' took place in the summer of 1958, although at least two were observed in January 1959. Even a 'D16' 4-4-0 was reported, heading an up freight in November 1959. One of the last Great Eastern 0-6-0s to be noted, 'J19' No 64655, came up with permanent way trains on successive Saturdays, 14 and 21 May 1960; on each occasion it returned a few days later on the 5.10am parcels to Baldock.

On the main line the changing pattern of motive power was more subtle, with various classes displaced by diesels and, in turn, displacing others. On such occasions as Bank Holidays and Rugby League

Above:
The heavy 5.52pm from King's Cross was regularly double-headed by a New England 'B1' and Cambridge 'Royal B2' No 61671 *Royal Sovereign* in the early part of 1958. 'B1' No 61302 is pilot as the train approaches Brookmans Park on 30 April and will take the last five coaches of the train from Hitchin to Peterborough, while the 'B2' returns home with the front six. *Royal Sovereign* was withdrawn five months later.
C. T. Gifford

Two unique Doncaster-based locomotives visited the 'Cross' almost daily for a number of years. *Below:* **The 'W1' No 60700, taking coal in 'Passenger Loco' on 15 July 1958, normally arrived on a morning York/ Hull express and returned with the 4.5pm to York/ Leeds.** *Bottom:* **'A1/1' No 60113 *Great Northern* passes Harringay with a down express in April 1960. The 'W1' was withdrawn in June 1959 and No 60113 in November 1962.** *Michael Joyce; D. I. D. Loveday*

Four tank engines find themselves on unfamiliar duties in 1958. *Below:* 'A5' No 69824 arrives at Hornsey with a train for Hertford during its brief spell on loan to Top Shed in February. *Right:* 'N2' No 69531 storms over the summit at Woolmer Green with the 4.45pm to Newcastle on 15 June; it had replaced a failed Pacific and worked the train as far as Hitchin. *Bottom:* 'C12' No 67352 came up from Grantham for an exhibition of locomotives and rolling stock at Noel Park. Next to the 4-4-2T on 13 September is 'J52' No 68846 (now preserved); both were repainted locally for the occasion. *D. I. D. Loveday; B. Coles (2)*

Cup Final weekends, when 'V2s' were formerly in great demand, there were enough spare Pacifics available by the early 1960s to handle the extra trains. Some classes, however, disappeared quickly. The 'W1' went in 1959, the six 'A2/2s' of York and New England were withdrawn by July 1961, while the only 'A2/1' in the area, New England's No 60508 *Duke of Rothesay*, was condemned in February of that year.

As the diesels arrived, in the summer of 1958, the motive power situation on main line expresses was at a particularly low ebb. 'V2s' frequently appeared in place of Pacifics on titled trains in July and the same month saw 'B1s' pressed into service. Saturdays found Top Shed at such a loss for something to work the 1.45pm Peterborough semi-fast and 1.52pm to

Leeds that 'K3s' and even '9Fs' were turned out. One of the 2-10-0s, No 92184 had to return from Grantham on 16 August with a passenger train — the 1.10pm from Edinburgh (not the 'Heart of Midlothian' as is usually related). After touching 90mph on the descent of Stoke Bank, the train ran through the area 6min early but lost most of that margin through signal checks approaching London. The following year saw more 'spaceships' on passenger duty — No 92141 with the 10.40am to Newcastle on 18 July and No 92041 with the 1.45pm on 15 August — while as late as Saturday 19 August 1961, another headed north on the 10.40am.

The summer of 1959 saw some unusual steam workings in place of diesels on suburban trains. Class 'N2' and even 'N7' 0-6-2Ts appeared on down

A variety of duties for three postwar Pacifics.
Above: **Peppercorn 'A2' No 60533** *Happy Knight*
**was allocated to Top Shed from June to December 1958
and, on 15 September (still with a Grantham shedplate)
worked the 4pm down 'Talisman' — one of the few
occasions an 'A2' took out this train.** *Left:*
Thompson 'A2/3' No 60524 *Herringbone* **passes Belle
Isle signalbox between the tunnels at King's Cross with
the 10.50am to Grantham on 8 September 1961.**
Below left: **'A1' No 60139** *Sea Eagle* **passes Langley
troughs with an up 'pick up' goods on 1 June 1963. The
troughs were removed in the summer of 1965.**
Michael Joyce; Colin Walker; D. Ludford

outer suburban services after the diesel that had
departed from King's Cross failed. Conversely, but
by design, Hitchin's 'B1s' and 'L1s' found themselves
on inner suburban trains earlier in the year, when
engineering work to upgrade the Hertford line for
70mph running involved off-peak closure of sections
and single-line operation in the 'peaks'. Each
morning, three groups of light engines travelled from
Hitchin to collect stock at various points on the
Loop for the morning commuter service, and the
process was reversed in the evening. Hatfield's
0-6-2Ts were also employed, travelling to and from
Hertford via the branch from Welwyn Garden City.
By the beginning of 1960, the only steam-hauled suburban train was the 7am from Cambridge (the
Cambridge-based locomotive returned on ECS, or
the 11.15am Broad Street-Hitchin on Saturdays). A
second turn, at 8.15am, joined the retimed 6.55am in

September but both were taken over by diesels in the following month.

An era ended at Hitchin in August 1960 when the depot's last 'B1s', Nos 61091/7, were transferred to New England. These two, and Nos 61090/3/4 (transferred away in 1959) had been allocated from new in the autumn of 1946. Their long service was well beaten by one of the 'J6s' transferred away in May 1960; No 64240 is believed to have served at the depot since 1923! Only three steam locomotives, all 'L1s', remained after August 1960 and they were moved to Top Shed by the end of November.

Hatfield shed, which provided locomotives primarily for the branch to Dunstable, closed at the beginning of 1961. Hornsey, meanwhile, was enjoying an Indian summer. Its allocation had been boosted by an influx of 'WDs' and its 'J50s' were constantly replenished after withdrawals. A Sunday morning visit in October 1960 found 60 locomotives on shed, of which 30 (half of the class at the time) were 'J50s'. Other locomotives present were 12 'WDs', six 'N2s', four 'J94s' and eight 350hp diesel shunters. The arrival of BR/Sulzer Type 2s, however, saw 13 of Hornsey's 36 'J50s' withdrawn and another 10 stored by the beginning of May 1961, and the depot lost its steam allocation two months later.

The summer of 1961 was the last in which the 'Elizabethan' was steam-hauled. King's Cross used 'A4s' Nos 60014/28 and Haymarket Nos 60024/31 for most of the season but the final northbound working, on Friday 8 September, was taken by No 60022 *Mallard* and the up train had No 60009 *Union of South Africa*. That same summer was the last opportunity to see most of the LNER Pacifics at King's Cross. In August alone, the author noted 26 out of 34 'A4s', 51 of the 76 existing 'A3s' and 35 of the 50 'A1s'.

During the early months of 1962, 'N2s' made their final appearances on ECS workings at the terminus, and the last five remaining in the area were transferred to New England towards the end of May. The last 'J50s' at King's Cross were withdrawn by the end of September. A 'K2' 2-6-0, No 61756, returned to the area during the year, but only as stationary boiler at Top Shed; it was replaced by 'K3' No 61912 in June 1962.

Those classes represented by occasional visitors were now being seen for the last time. In January 1962 a Grantham 'O2' appeared, and a York 'B16' was seen in October. Great Eastern 0-6-0s made one or two visits and Scottish Pacifics of all four LNER types were noted during the year. 'Britannias' ended their run on the Cleethorpes trains in November and the first five 'A4s' were withdrawn, from King's Cross, at the end of the year (Nos 60003/14/28/30/3). The steam-heating boilers of Brush Type 2 diesels seemed unable to cope with the winter of 1962/3,

and 'B1s' deputised on empty stock workings; one of them was a rare named example, No 61010 *Wildebeeste*, based at Hull Dairycoates, which remained in the area for a time during the autumn. The severe weather lasting until March 1963 gave 'B1s' a final opportunity to stretch their legs on the 'Cambridge Buffet Express' and other suburban passenger services. The 8.22am Hatfield-King's Cross was even Pacific-hauled more than once, while withdrawn 'A3' No 60109 *Hermit* was employed on carriage-heating duties in February and March. During the same period, ECS workings to and from the terminus featured such unusual power as 'V2s' and New England based LMS Ivatt '4' 2-6-0s.

As the run down of Top Shed's Pacifics continued, No 60103 *Flying Scotsman* made its last run before being bought for preservation, to Doncaster with the 1.15pm King's Cross-Leeds, on 14 January. The Easter and Whitsun Bank Holidays gave steam its last fling on the southern end of the East Coast main line. Almost half (51 out of 104) of the main line passenger services observed on Maundy Thursday were steam-hauled, and Easter Monday afternoon saw a procession of Pacifics arriving on regular and relief trains.

During the last few weeks before the official end of steam in mid-June, Top Shed's remaining Pacifics began to appear travel-worn for the first time in a decade, although they performed as well as ever. In the six weeks from 1 May only about a dozen failures in traffic were attributable to the 11 'A4s' and six 'A3s'. As the last day drew near, the 'gallery' on Platform 10 every evening admired steam departures at 6.12, 6.17, 6.26 and 6.32 (parcels) and the incoming 'Northumbrian' and 'White Rose'. The last few notable 'foreigners' reached the area in the shape of 'O4s' Nos 63628 and 63788, Stanier '8F' No 48614 and Aston-based 'Britannia' No 70028 in May and 'Jubilee' No 45597 with a special from Bradford on 8 June.

On the morning of 15 June, the departure of stationary boiler No 61912, hauled by No 60112 *St Simon*, signalled the end for Top Shed. The last scheduled steam-hauled train out of King's Cross on Sunday 16 June was the 10.45pm to Leeds, hauled by 'A1' No 60158 *Aberdonian*.

Monday 17 June dawned steamless but by the following morning '9F' No 92146 had found its way to Hornsey and later that day 'B1' No 61122 came up with a freight. Steam was allowed to work south to Hitchin, normally 'B1s' or '9Fs' on an early morning and an afternoon freight. Also steam-powered was the 12.56am parcels from York, booked for a Pacific to Hitchin and generally worked by 'A4s' until they moved from New England in October.

Up to the end of June, most steam locomotives penetrating south of Hitchin were '9Fs' (particularly

Nos 92144/6) on freights, but soon Pacific-hauled expresses were travelling through. It was then only a matter of time before they were appropriated for the evening York parcels, northbound express freights and, eventually, passenger services. By the autumn, several steam locomotives were reaching London daily. On 29 October, five worked through Stevenage between 7pm and 7.30pm, including 'A1' No 60117 with the up 'White Rose' and 'A4' No 60017 — withdrawn nine days before! — on the 6.40pm to Leeds. Three titled trains came up behind Pacifics on 9 December — the 'Aberdonian' ('A1' No 60138), 'Flying Scotsman' ('A3' No 60106) and 'Northumbrian' ('A3' No 60063).

Steam workings declined after coal, water and oil supplies to Top Shed were discontinued and the depot was physically isolated on 13 January 1964. Rumour has it that 'A1' No 60141 was on shed while track was being lifted! Another 'A1', No 60114 distinguished itself on 4 April, bringing the 'Yorkshire Pullman' from Doncaster in 150min and making up 8min on the schedule.

During February, March and April 1964, workings were mostly confined to 'B1s' involved in steam-heating duties at Holloway carriage sidings; one of them, No 61109, was removed from an up freight to work the 8.22am Hatfield-King's Cross on 6 April.

Steam locomotive sightings continued for more than a year after steam was officially banned from the 'Cross'. The closing months of 1964 produced 'A3s' Nos 60063 and 60112, 'A1' No 60149 and a sprinkling of 'B1s' and '9Fs'. Frodingham 'WD' No 90053 and Retford 'O4' No 63607 appeared north of Hitchin at the end of the year. Subsequent special workings apart, the last steam locomotive seen in the vicinity of King's Cross seems to have been 'B1' No 61070, observed at Finsbury Park diesel depot on New Year's Day 1965.

5

The Diesel Locomotive Era

Diesel locomotives reigned for some 15 years, from June 1963 until completion of suburban electrification in February 1978 and the introduction of High Speed Trains on the main ECML expresses three months later. Throughout the period, the bulk of locomotive-hauled work was handled by Class 55 'Deltics' and Brush Type 4s (Class 47) and Type 2s (Class 31).

Interest in the early years centred on the performance of two prototype locomotives. First of the pair was English Electric's 2,700bhp Co-Co No DP2, which arrived in mid-July 1963. For eight weeks continuously it worked the 10.10am to Edinburgh and returned overnight on the 10.30pm, arriving at 5.24am, on Mondays to Saturdays. On at least two occasions it also worked the Sunday 5.10pm to Newcastle and returned overnight for Monday's 10.10am

Towards the end of this remarkable run, the white-liveried BRCW 2,750bhp prototype No D0260 *Lion* began a diagram involving a return trip to Leeds and another to Grantham each day. Relieved at the end of September by No DP2, *Lion* moved on to Sheffield Pullman duties but after a series of failures it left the area early in February 1964. Once more, No DP2 followed in its footsteps and worked the Pullmans throughout 1964, suffering its only failure *en route* on 3 September. In 1965 it returned to English Electric for overhaul, reappearing in 'Deltic' livery in August to resume its Sheffield Pullman duties. From October it was officially on hire to Finsbury Park depot and, late in November, it reverted to the Leeds and Grantham trip. Early in 1966 No DP2 went back to the manufacturer again for modifications and in mid-June it took up work on the down 'Car Sleeper Limited' and up 'Anglo-Scottish Car Carrier' between King's Cross and Edinburgh. A spell on the 'Cambridge Buffet Express' and a York return trip each day in October and November was followed by more Edinburgh trips in 1967, working the down 'Flying Scotsman' on occasion. On 31 July 1967 No DP2 left King's

Cross for the last time, with the 12.00 to Aberdeen; near Thirsk it ran into a derailed cement train and sustained damage that led to its withdrawal. A sad end to a highly successful career.

A further prototype appeared briefly two years later. The 4,000bhp Brush Co-Co No HS4000 *Kestrel* arrived early in October 1969 and after some trial runs to Peterborough took up duty on the 07.55 to Newcastle and 16.45 return on 22 October. After four weeks *Kestrel* resumed its former work on Shirebrook-Whitemoor freights.

To return to the early years of the diesel era, observers in the King's Cross area soon became accustomed to seeing Brush Type 4s and 'Peaks' from the Western and Midland Regions, and English Electric Type 4s from the Midland, as standardisation of motive power types spread through the BR system. Interest in the new form of traction also increased as unusual pairings of types were recorded. In December 1963 these included an English Electric Type 1 and a Brush Type 4 on a Glasgow train, and a BR/Sulzer Type 2 piloting a 'Peak' on the up 'Northumbrian', while on 9 April 1964 Type 1 No D8020 was commandeered from a Hitchin-Hertford freight to assist 'Deltic' No D9020 with the up 'Night Scotsman'.

Early in 1964 the first Brush Type 2 was re-engined with an English Electric engine; No D5677 was transferred from Finsbury Park to Tinsley in November and was soon a regular performer on the Cleethorpes-King's Cross trains. 'Deltics' made appearances on freight workings in 1965, including No D9010 (18 September) and another (1 November) on the afternoon Scottish freight.

Tinsley Type 4s took over the Sheffield Pullmans at the beginning of the summer 1965 timetable; generally the latest batch commencing with No D1862 was used. One of the diagrams covered the 11.20 and 19.10 'Master Cutler' from King's Cross, balanced by the 15.25 from Sheffield and an up overnight freight, but the other was particularly

interesting as the Type 4 spent part of its time on suburban passenger services. The locomotive arrived with the 'Master Cutler' then took the 14.35 to Royston, 16.24 Royston-Cambridge, 17.10 to King's Cross and 20.50 King's Cross Goods-Sheffield (later the 21.05 to Tinsley) fitted freight. An alternative suburban trip was the 15.30 to Baldock and 17.05 return.

An English Electric Type 3 with central headcode panel was seen for the first time at the 'Cross' on 24 July, when No D6961 of Darnall brought in the 10.00 (SO) from Leeds and returned north on the 20.35 parcels to York. It was one of six Type 3s seen that day, the others being No D6721 of Stratford on a petrol train and Darnall's Nos D6797 and D6800 on the two Cleethorpes workings, No D6744 on the 13.40 to Leeds, and No D6742 piloting Type 4 No D1870 on the 11.50 to Hull. Double-heading was a frequent occurrence in the summer, with pairs of Brush Type 2s noted on Peterborough, Hull and Cleethorpes services.

Haymarket's new Class 47s (Nos D1968-76) began working regularly to London at the end of the year, particularly on the overnight 19.15 from

Aberdeen. Gateshead's Nos D1977-89 also appeared from mid-December; one of their duties was the 10.15 from Newcastle and the 18.05 down 'North Eastern'. The trio of Holbeck Class 47s, Nos D1765-7, were frequent visitors in the early part of 1966 with the 07.50 and 12.20 from Leeds, returning at 15.20 and 18.40.

From April 1966, both Sheffield Pullman diagrams were taken over by Finsbury Park Type 4s. Tinsley's gained the Cleethorpes turns, but were later displaced by Immingham Type 4s. As in the two previous years, Maundy Thursday was notable for the double-heading of up expresses, bringing locomotives to London for northbound 'extras'. In 1966 there were four such pairings: Nos D1506 and D1534, D1550 and D9019, D1517 and D1767, and D1529 and D1536.

Visitors during the year included LMR 'Peaks' — especially on the Sheffield Pullman workings which, since October 1965, were running to and from Sheffield Midland instead of Victoria; BR/Sulzer Type 2s from the GE section on suburban passenger workings; and EE Type 3s from the north-east on freight and parcels trains — often returning on the early evening parcels to York. Western Region EE Type 3s and Brush Type 4s also found themselves on ECML workings after bringing inter-regional freights to Temple Mills or York.

Late in 1966 a more unusual type appeared, the BR/Sulzer 1,250bhp Type 2 (Class 25); No D7606

Below:
**Class 31s Nos 31.222 and 31.209 are working in
multiple on the 13.35 (SO) Skegness-King's Cross,
leaving Welwyn North Tunnel on 10 August 1974.
Although electrification masts are in position, the wiring
train has not yet reached this part of the line.**
David Percival

Bottom:
**On the first day of its 91.3mph timing to Retford,
14 May 1979, the 17.05 down 'Hull Executive' storms
through Oakleigh Park in the charge of 'white-cab'
'Deltic' No 55.003 *Meld*.** *Keith Grafton*

At the beginning of the diesel era, the six types of locomotive illustrated handled virtually all main line services out of King's Cross. *Top:* **Brush Type 4 No D1506 is ready to depart with the 6.12pm for York and Hull on 20 June 1963 as an EE Type 4 propels a parcels van into Platform 11. In the loco yard are a 'Deltic' and an EE Type 3 — No D6818 — which will work the 6.45pm to Cleethorpes.** *Above:* **On 22 June 1963, Brush Type 2 No D5675 hauls an up train of petrol tanks through Knebworth.** *Right:* **The 3pm to Newcastle, headed by 'Peak' No D181, approaches Sandy on 17 August 1963.** *David Percival (2); C. Burton*

of Barrow Hill spent the last part of November stabled in the yard at Finsbury Park depot and Haymarket's No D7603 came up with a parcels train on 22 December. One of the earlier BR/Sulzer Type 2s, No D5005 of Bletchley, in two-tone livery, was observed on Sunday engineering duty at Wood Green on 13 November.

The change to blue livery began to make itself apparent late in 1966. Among the first of their respective classes seen in the area were Nos D173, D5649 and D9002. Those locomotives visiting works but not fully repainted were turned out in their original livery but with full yellow ends and, in most cases, new-style numerals.

In September 1967, Tinsley's 'vee'-engined Brush Type 4s Nos D1702-6 (later Class 48) began to work regularly to London, usually on the 17.50 from Leeds, returning next morning on the 10.20. The following summer saw them on the Sheffield

Pullmans, but their reign was short-lived as the service was withdrawn in October.

The transfer of some 'Peaks' from the Midland line to Holbeck at the end of 1967 brought some unfamiliar numbers to King's Cross regularly on Leeds expresses — Nos D139/48/53/60/64 were the locomotives involved.

New classifications for diesel locomotive classes were introduced in 1968 and in August of that year, when the last BR main line steam locomotives were withdrawn, the 'D' prefix for diesel locomotive numbers was discontinued. In later years, 1973/4 saw a complete renumbering to the now familiar TOPS system, by which time most of the locomotives seen in the area had received their blue livery. However, some visiting Class 47s and local Class 08s were still green even at that late stage.

A diagram introduced in May 1969 brought a Tinsley Class 31 to a King's Cross-Welwyn Garden

City service in an unusual working which is worth noting in full. The locomotive came to London on the 22.45 Tinsley-Temple Mills freight, ran light engine to Finsbury Park, then worked ECS from Ferme Park to Finsbury Park carriage sidings. It then ran light engine to Waterworks sidings, standing pilot there until 16.00 and taking the 16.55 ECS from Bounds Green to King's Cross. A passenger trip followed, on the 18.04 to Welwyn Garden City and 19.41 return, after which the Class 31 ran light engine to King's Cross Goods, took the 21.05 Bradford parcels as far as Doncaster and returned light to Tinsley.

Among the 'visitors' in 1969 were Dairycoates Class 37s, two of which — Nos 6732/81 — double-headed the 8.55 Hull-King's Cross on 23 August. On 8 September No 6740 came up with the 'Hull Pullman' and returned (as did No 6781 on 23 August) on the 14.20 to York. The transfer of named Class 47s Nos 1665/6/72 from the Western Region to Stratford in the summer brought them to the GN line on Tilbury-Royston petrol trains.

Class 31s began to appear on main line passenger trains in greater numbers from 1970 onwards. In that year such trains as the 07.25 from Lincoln, 16.30 from Doncaster and some Cleethorpes services featured pairs of these locomotives from time to time. Since the transfer away of Finsbury Park's Class 20s in 1966 the type had made sporadic visits, but York-based examples passed through quite frequently in the early 1970s, taking locomotives to or from Stratford Works. One of the final series, No 8305, travelled up light engine on 10 November 1970 and returned north hauling Class 37 No 6968.

Diesel locomotive renumbering began in 1973 and No 47.168 (formerly 1763) is believed to have been the first renumbered locomotive observed in the area when it travelled up light engine with Class 24 No 5111 of Gateshead on 7 September. Several Class 25s penetrated the area during the year, including No 5283 piloting Class 47 No 1963 on the 06.00 from Cleethorpes on 6 June, Nos 7608 and 5190 double-heading the 06.30 from Peterborough on 2 August and Nos 5223/5 with an up excursion on 8 September. Class 25s occasionally brought ballast trains up to the permanent way yard at Hitchin (in later years there was a regular thrice-weekly working from Nuneaton), or appeared on the 06.43 semi-fast from Peterborough.

Left:
'Passenger Loco' on 14 September 1970 is monopolised by Class 47s in both original and blue liveries. Nos 1542 and 1515 are nearest the camera. The new signalbox is under construction behind the York Road platform. 'Passenger loco' closed in May 1979. *BR, Eastern Region*

By the spring of 1974, renumbering of locomotives was virtually complete although, on 21 March, Class 40 No 314 of Longsight and '47' No 1962 of Bescot were noted on freights. Among the more unusual locomotive pairings during the summer were Nos 37.194 of Thornaby and 55.004 on the 08.55 from Aberdeen on 19 June (Nos 46.037 and 55.004 headed the same train on 23 January 1975), and Nos 45.011 of Holbeck and 55.005 with the up 'Yorkshire Pullman' on 27 September. Class 45s were infrequent visitors, although No 45.116 of Toton and unrenumbered No 48 of Holbeck were observed on 22 October, while Toton's No 45.123 appeared on the following day's 12.30 from Leeds. On 27 November the 12.30 again had a Toton '45', No 45.128, and No 45.007 of Holbeck was seen the same day.

Regular multiple-workings of Class 31s in 1975 included the 06.43 from Peterborough; on 12 March, however, the train had Nos 31.185 and 25.037. Toton '25s' regularly reached King's Cross with ECS for the 15.05 (FO) to Leeds in February and March. At least 20 Western Region Class 46s were observed at King's Cross during 1975 while the following two years saw Class 45s — mostly from Holbeck — arriving in greater numbers, and often working the 14.45 and 19.50 to Newcastle, both Fridays Only services.

A green '40' was seen after a lapse of time when No 40.136 came up on 22 August 1976 and worked the next evening's Edinburgh parcels. Just over a month later No 47.195 appeared; the same locomotive — still green — was seen again in April 1977. At the beginning of 1977, Doncaster Works gained responsibility for the overhaul of Class 50s and the first to be dealt with, No 50.009, spent the night of 30 December 1976 on Finsbury Park depot before being towed north by No 37.055 next day. It reappeared in unusual circumstances on 16 June 1977 when, newly ex-Works, it brought an express to King's Cross after another locomotive had failed. Subsequently several '50s' have been observed running light engine to or from Doncaster via the GN line and, occasionally, on express passenger duty.

Perhaps the most unusual of all diesel visitors was No 44.005 *Cross Fell* on 11 May 1977. Believed to be the only Class 44 ever seen in the area, it brought a train of empty coaching stock from the LMR to Bounds Green and returned north light engine. Another 'first' occurred on 2 August 1977, when Toton's No 56.031 called at Finsbury Park depot *en route* between the LMR and Stratford. The depot also saw Tinsley's No 56.001 on 14 November 1977 and No 56.018 travelled up light engine on 12 July 1979 for an 'open day' at Stratford two days later.

A nostalgic moment on Saturday 6 May 1978 was the departure of the last locomotive-hauled 'Flying Scotsman'; HSTs took over on the following Monday. Compared with No D9020's sparkling appearance on the first 'six hour' departure 16 years

In 1963, the English Electric prototype No DP2 began four successful years' work on the ECML. *Left:* Its earliest duties included the 10.10am to Edinburgh, with which it is departing on 10 August 1963; BR Type 2 No D5067 and a Paxman Type 1 are on pilot duty. Much less impressive was the BRCW prototype No D0260 *Lion,* whose white livery was the only outstanding feature. *Below: Lion* heads the up 'Yorkshire Pullman'

around the curves at Offord on 9 September 1963. Six years later, the Brush 4,000bhp locomotive, No HS4000 *Kestrel* briefly appeared on ECML passenger service. *Bottom:* At Clarence Yard on 7 October 1969, *Kestrel* is coupled to stock for a test of its ETH equipment; LMR Class 25 No D5216 waits for the road as Class 31 No D5598 passes with a down empty stock train. *David Percival; BR, Eastern Region; Peter Foster*

before, 'Deltic' No 55.010 was given no special treatment. In spite of its unkempt appearance, the 'Deltics' were were not quite ready to bow out. They continued to be very much in evidence and on the August Bank Holiday Monday made at least a dozen departures from King's Cross — at a time when the Editor of one national railway magazine was busily writing off the class! In the spring of 1979 the Gateshead and Haymarket '55s' were transferred to York; Finsbury Park, meanwhile, began painting the cab roofs and window surrounds white on their 'racehorses'. The 91.3mph sprint to Retford of the down 'Hull Executive' in 1979/80 was a high spot of their career, as was the repainting green of

No 55.002 in December 1980. But Nos 55.001/20 were withdrawn at the end of 1979 and in two years the class became extinct. Their working of the York and Hull trains, though, was not without interest and on two or three occasions in 1980/1 double-headed 'Deltics' graced these services. In their final weeks, a few enthusiasts' specials ran behind 'Deltics' from King's Cross, the last being on 2 January 1982 when the 'Deltic Scotsman Farewell' ran to Edinburgh behind No 55.015 and returned with No 55.022.

The last service trains hauled by 'Deltics' to or from the 'Cross' ran on 31 December 1981: the 09.40 to York (No 55.021); 16.03 to York (No 55.017) which terminated at Grantham and returned as an 'extra' as far as Knebworth where the 'Deltic' failed; and the 15.50 from York (No 55.015).

The loss of these ECML named locomotives was made good with the less extravagant naming of a batch of Gateshead '47s', Nos 47401-6, commencing late in 1981 with No 47.402 *Gateshead.*

Finsbury Park's main line diesels were transferred away at the end of May 1981, from which date March and York '31s' and York and Gateshead '47s' have been the mainstay of locomotive-hauled services. In the following year it was the turn of '40s' and '46s' to excite the interest of observers at King's Cross. All the remaining '46s' appeared during 1982, but both classes are now rarely seen. Until its withdrawal, green-liveried No 40.106 appeared on several occasions after its Crewe Works repaint late in 1978.

Only one York and one Cleethorpes service in each direction were locomotive hauled at the beginning of 1982. The former became an HST working in May and the latter in October. Diesel locomotives now remain only on Peterborough semi-fasts and overnight trains, with their associated ECS workings, and the sparse freight and parcels services.

Visits by other regions' locomotives occasionally make a welcome change from the types normally seen in the area. *Right:* **After bringing a cross-London freight, Southern Region electro-diesel (later Class 73) No E6040 crosses the Ferme Park flyover on 7 January 1967. The first Class 50 to reach the 'Cross' was No 50.009 with the 08.30 from Leeds on 16 June 1977.** *Below:* **Local railwaymen show interest as it waits to return with the 14.10 to Leeds. Due to blockage of the Midland line on 2 June 1981, St Pancras trains ran to and from King's Cross.** *Bottom:* **Class 45 No 45.125 comes down the bank at Holloway with one of the diverted expresses.** *David Percival (2); Brian Morrison*

6

Diesel Multiple-Units

Lineside observers in the King's Cross area on 1 August 1958 were more than a little startled to see an eight-car formation of diesel multiple-units heading south in the early afternoon. The only DMUs seen before had been two-car Derby-built units on driver-training trips for short periods in 1956 and on AWS trials early in 1958, and an experimental two-car unit which came up to King's Cross twice in October 1957. But on this Friday before the Bank Holiday weekend four pairs of Cravens twins, based at Lincoln, were sent up to form a Cleethorpes relief at 3.59pm, the first public DMU service from the terminus. Next day the same rake, plus another twin, formed the 6.30am from Cleethorpes and 3.52pm return.

The Cravens unit was soon to be a familiar sight in the area and remain so for the next 20 years. Transferred from Lincoln to Cambridge, they were employed during the late summer and autumn on Sunday shuttle services between Potters Bar and Stevenage, resulting from quadrupling work at Hadley Wood and Potters Bar, and were soon at work on some inner suburban services. From

February 1959 they also took over some outer suburban turns.

A minor change in appearance came in 1960 when the 'vee' styling flash beneath the cab windows was replaced by a more functional yellow panel. In that year other types of unit began to appear in the area. On 29 July, for instance, a Wickham pair (Nos E50416-56171) combined with a Cravens twin on the 9.08pm from Cambridge. And on 25 September a four-car Marylebone unit (some of which were on loan to the GE at that time) was observed travelling up empty through Stevenage.

Of more significance was the transfer of the Cravens units in April 1960 to Finsbury Park, where they were stabled in the former Western Sidings

Below:
The unusual sight of a lengthy diesel unit tests a spotter's ability at Hitchin on 1 August 1958. The eight-car rake of Cravens units formed the first public DMU service from King's Cross when it departed as an afternoon 'relief' to Cleethorpes. 'B1' No 61364 is visible in the locomotive depot. *Michael Joyce*

carriage shed near the diesel depot. Maintenance continued to be carried out at Cambridge and the diagrams allowed each unit to make periodic visits for the purpose. New work for DMUs, from September 1962, included Dunstable branch and some Huntingdon/Peterborough services.

By the mid-1960s, Wickham units were appearing occasionally in some of the diagrams which had been introduced for Cambridge-based units. One of these units, Nos E50416-56171, was converted to General Manager's Saloon early in 1966 and repainted blue with the BR 'double arrow' symbol as a chromed plate. In this condition it was noted in the King's Cross area on 12 May.

Express diesel units from other regions made trial runs through the area on two occasions in the late 1960s. Completion of Euston-Manchester electrification in May 1966 was to make the St Pancras-Manchester 'Midland Pullman' redundant, and thought was given to transferring the units to an East Coast Pullman service. So, on 16 October 1965 a six-car 'Midland Pullman' unit ran from Leeds to King's Cross and back. In the event the idea was abandoned and the units were later transferred to the Western Region.

Hastings line six-car unit No 1001 travelled on the GN line in the course of a test run to and from Grantham on 6 January 1968, following concern

that poor riding of the stock had contributed to a derailment at Hither Green two months earlier. In the early 1970s, units of this type again travelled over East Coast metals on excursion trips from the South Coast to the Lincolnshire bulbfields.

The late-1960s saw new types of DMU at work in the area. In April 1966, five of the older Cravens twins, without the two-character headcode panel, were transferred to Finsbury Park from Cambridge (where they had arrived a few months earlier from Hull). In the next two years, however, a more distinctive DMU variation appeared, in the shape of three-car Derby-built suburban or 'high density' units, of two types. Four BUT-engined (later

Class 116) units, originally from the Western Region, were moved from South Gosforth to Finsbury Park in June/July 1968 for outer suburban duties. In part they helped fill the shortage of power caused by withdrawal of the 'Baby Deltics'. At first they were employed as three or six-car trains but in later years they combined with Cravens units on some workings. Indeed, the non-availability of one of their power cars often resulted in substitution by a Cravens motor brake second, forming a hybrid unit.

The other suburban type was a Rolls-Royce engined version (later Class 125), displaced from the Liverpool Street suburban lines by extension of electrification. From May 1969 these were introduced on

Above left:
In the spring of 1969, when repairs were being carried out to the stabling shed at Western Sidings, Finsbury Park's DMUs were 'evacuated' to Hornsey, where Cravens and Derby units are on view on 22 March.
David Percival

Left:
Metro-Cammell Class 101 unit (its trailer car No E56057 at that time classified 144) leaves Cambridge as the 11.05 service to Royston in March 1978. *I. J. Hodson*

Top:
Empty stock for the 11.44 (SO) Moorgate-Hatfield approaches Farringdon on 15 October 1960, with its leading unit displaying the yellow 'whisker'. The diesel shunter in the spur was employed to bank freights bound for the Southern Region on the gradient to Holborn Viaduct. *J. C. Beckett*

Above:
One of the earlier Cravens units without headcode panels forms the 15.18 Huntingdon-Finsbury Park service on 28 March 1972. The unit is passing a down freight north of Sandy. *Dr R. Elsdon*

inner suburban services. One six-car formation was booked to reach Hitchin as the 17.17 from Broad Street via Hertford and return next morning as the 05.26 to King's Cross, but it was not long before the units made more frequent appearances in the outer suburban area. Higher powered than the BUT-engined units, they were well-suited to inner suburban work and noticeably quicker off the mark on outer suburban turns, though the lack of toilet facilities — as with the BUT variety — was a disadvantage on the longer workings.

During 1970, Metro-Cammell, Wickham and Gloucester RCW twin units provided occasional variety in dmu formations, and a Birmingham RCW three-car unit (Nos E50549-59213-50570) also appeared, on 6 May. An unusual diagram in 1971 involved a Cambridge-based formation — normally two twin units — working the 10.50 (SO) to King's Cross and then providing a through service at 10.34 to Harwich, via Cambridge. Rolls-Royce-engined units gained a booked working on the Cambridge branch from July 1972, with the 07.24 King's Cross-Royston and 09.17 return.

Visits of the Wickham General Manager's Saloon, renumbered DB975005/6, continued throughout the decade and the area saw several more Departmental units including the ultrasonic track testing unit (Nos DB975007/8), test car *Iris* (No DB975010) and route-learning car No TDB975309 which was based at Finsbury Park in the late-1970s.

Above:

In September 1958, Park Royal railbuses took over the LMR passenger service from Bedford to Hitchin, where No M79971 is seen on 13 March 1959. By the end of that year, two-car DMUs were being employed and even steam push-pull operation had returned. *Michael Joyce*

Left:

The 'Midland Pullman' is about mid-way through its two-hour visit to King's Cross on 16 October 1965. The six-car unit, with power cars Nos M60090/1, was making a return trial run from Leeds. *BR, Eastern Region*

Below left:

Hastings unit No 1001 passes Woolmer Green during a test run to Grantham on 6 January 1968. The unit returned the same day. *David Percival*

A small, but noticeable, modification to the Cravens units was the removal of the two-character headcode panels, carried out from early 1976. May of that year saw the introduction of a working which brought a Norwich-based unit to King's Cross each day, on the 22.25 from Cambridge and returning the following morning at 06.30. Cravens units were normally employed, but Gloucester twins and BRCW twin and three-car units were also used.

Electrification of suburban services in the late 1970s virtually brought an end to DMU working in the area. The Class 125 units, made redundant in November 1976, were put into store (mostly at Finsbury Park and Stratford) and withdrawn during the next three months. The release of Cravens units from inner suburban workings resulted in longer outer suburban formations during the next year or so.

From September 1977, Metro-Cammell units (Class 101), newly-refurbished and in the short-lived white livery with broad blue band, arrived on outer suburban workings. Eight pairs were transferred to Cambridge — to provide the Royston-Cambridge and Hertford-Huntingdon/Peterborough shuttle services connecting with the new outer suburban electrics — by February 1978. In that month the Derby/BUT three-car units were transferred from Finsbury Park to Tyseley and the Cravens units were dispersed to various Eastern Region depots. The Metro-Cammell units' sphere of operations was reduced in May 1979 when the Huntingdon-Hertford shuttle was cut back to Hitchin.

During the ASLEF strike in July 1982, DMUs once again came to King's Cross daily, operating a handful of services to and from Peterborough — or even further north. Most of them were Metro-Cammell twin or three-car units, but Derby 'heavyweight' twins (Class 114) and Swindon Cross-country three-car units (Class 120) also appeared. One formation, on 13 July, was of 12 cars — probably the longest train of DMUs ever to have departed on a passenger service from the 'Cross'.

At the end of the year, the sight of a Cravens twin at Finsbury Park depot recalled memories. But the unit was merely stabled there between route-learning trips in preparation for the daily transfer of HSTs to and from the Midland line. Since they deputise from time to time for Metro-Cammell units on the shuttle services, it is still possible to see Cravens units at work in the King's Cross area after a quarter of a century of more or less continuous service.

7

Coaching Stock

A quarter of a century ago, variations in the formation of main line trains seen at King's Cross were almost as numerous as the trains themselves. The prestige services were formed mainly of BR Standard Mk I stock, with LNER catering vehicles, but many trains contained a high proportion of both Gresley and Thompson LNER coaches. Train lengths and formations suited the requirements of the one service — or two at most — which the sets covered each day, and extra coaches were added as necessary. There was were no 'standard' formation or intensive diagramming.

Suburban trains, too, included BR and LNER stock. Non-corridor vehicles of Gresley design, however, were seen mostly on Dunstable branch trains and in the eight-coach trains of 'Quad Arts'. Most trains conformed to standard lengths, such as the inner suburban five-coach sets of BR non-gangwayed stock and corridor trains on the Cam-

Below:
At the south end of the 'Elizabethan' was one of the three full brakes built for the 'Flying Scotsman' in 1947 and much of the train was of the same vintage, identified by the covered solebars. The second vehicle is a corridor first with ladies' retiring room. A permanent way worker admires the ensemble as it passes Hitchin on 2 August 1960, hauled by Haymarket 'A4' No 60027 *Merlin*. *Michael Joyce*

bridge service which were formed of three BR open seconds and a Thompson compartment first with a Gresley brake second at each end.

Repainting in maroon livery had commenced in 1956 but 'blood and custard' was much in evidence in 1958 and survived for another three years, along with non-gangwayed stock in unlined red livery. A further variation in colour was provided by Pullman trains, all formed of traditional stock in umber and cream.

With the possible exception of the Pullmans, the most distinctive and handsome main line formations were seen on the 'Talisman' and 'Elizabethan' — most of the latter's stock operating during the winter months on the 'Flying Scotsman'. Normally, the 'Talisman' was an eight-coach rake, with four BR vehicles, Thompson kitchen/restaurant and restaurant open second, and an articulated twin open first from the prewar 'Coronation' express; the mix sounds curious but the ensemble made an impressive sight. The 'Elizabethan' was formed almost entirely of stock built in 1947 for the 'Scotsman', including a first and a second each with a 'ladies retiring room'. At the south end of the train was one of the trio of full brakes of the same vintage (Nos E10-12E) which looked particularly well in lined maroon livery.

A curious spectacle was presented by the early evening 'sleeper', then departing at 7.45pm, often with a couple of four or six-wheeled parcels vans next to the locomotive, portions for Aberdeen, Elgin and Fort William (those for Aberdeen and Fort William including sleeping cars) and a restaurant car on the rear. The last vehicle was detached at York and for some years was Gresley kitchen/restaurant No SC9023E, although prototype car No E1700 was used for a period in 1960.

In September 1958 a new six-car Pullman formation was introduced, for the Sheffield 'Master Cutler' service. Two years later the first of 44 new Pullman Cars for East Coast services were delivered and the 'Cutler' was the first train to be re-equipped, on 28 September 1960. Replacement of older cars in the other Pullmans took place early in 1961. The new stock comprised only Kitchen and Parlour Cars, plus a replacement *Hadrian Bar* for the 'Tees-Tyne'. Existing or remodelled brake seconds completed the new trains, but during the 1960s they were replaced by Standard full brakes.

By the beginning of the decade, new restaurant and buffet cars were replacing LNER catering vehicles on ECML services. Miniature buffet cars (RMBs) Nos E1801-12 had appeared in 1958 (the first of them entering service in the 'Scotsman' in January) and further buffet and unclassed restaurant cars were introduced in the next two years. Among the casualties were the Gresley restaurant car

triplets, the earliest of them dating from 1924. These articulated sets were formed restaurant first/kitchen/ restaurant second and their passage in a train was marked by the distinctive rhythm of their wheels on the rail joints. In two of the sets, the restaurant first had been modified to include a bar during the 1950s and these sets operated in the 'Northumbrian' during the winter 1959/60 timetable. Another triplet was still in service on the 9.55am from Newcastle and 5.35pm return, but all were replaced by the end of 1960.

Minor changes in the appearance of coaching stock in 1962 included maroon-painted ends on some standard coaches and the fitting of various types of Continental bogies to open second No E4723 and composites Nos E16015/25, which were in ECML service. Towards the end of the year, yellow bands began to be painted above the windows of first class accommodation; standard SLF No E2061 was one of the first coaches seen at King's Cross with this treatment, early in November.

An interesting diagram involving the 'Flying Scotsman' was in operation at this time. The set working the down train returned next day as the 'Heart of Midlothian' and went north again as the 'Scotsman' on the third day, but that which arrived on the up train included a Newcastle trip in its two-day roster. After reaching London at 4pm it was turned round for the 5.35pm to Newcastle, returned next day as the 7.50am (arriving at 12.05pm), departed as the 2pm 'Midlothian' and covered the up 'Scotsman' again on the third day. Thus four sets were used on six trains each day, resulting in the saving of the stock formerly used for the Newcastle return trip.

In February 1964, two of the three prototype griddle cars — Nos M1100 and W1101 — came to the East Coast route, and were installed in the sets working the down 'Scotsman'/up 'Midlothian'. These trains were among the first, in June, to receive the new Mk II coaches, corridor firsts Nos E13361-78.

By 1964, ordinary Gresley stock was becoming scarce, but a presentable nine-coach formation of open seconds and open brake seconds, together with buffet car No E1852E, was made up for the 'London North Eastern Flier' railtour, worked to York and back by 'A3' No 60106 on 2 May. A week later the set was employed on a Lincolnshire bulbfields excursion, strengthened with two standard open seconds and with a miniature buffet in place of the Gresley car.

The most eye-catching of the year's coaching stock developments was the 'XP64' set, introduced on the up morning and down afternoon 'Talisman'.

LNER articulated main line stock ended its days in the early 1960s. *Above:* **One of the prewar 'Coronation' open first twins, Nos E1713/4E, stands at the back of Bounds Green 'shops' on 7 April 1962 after service on the 'Talisman' since 1956.** *Below:* **A steel-panelled BSK-SK twin, of the type built for Peterborough-King's** Cross and other semi-fast services in the late 1930s and early 1940s, is coupled behind a grimy 'V2' on a down Whitsun Holiday 'extra', emerging from Hadley Wood North Tunnel on 31 May 1963.
David Percival; Brian Haresnape

Above:
Thompson non-gangwayed lavatory composites Nos E88412E and E88550E in an outer suburban formation at Knebworth on 27 October 1962. *David Percival*

examples repainted in two-tone livery.
BR, Eastern Region

Bottom:
Gresley and Thompson buffet cars outlasted other LNER passenger-carrying stock and some survived to be repainted blue-and-grey. Gresley buffet No E9129E is included in the Class 47-hauled 08.26 from Cleethorpes, heading towards Langley Junction on 9 March 1968. *David Percival*

Below:
Bounds Green carriage sidings on 3 January 1966. The Brush Type 2 in the foreground is No D5673, fitted with tablet catcher, and the BR/Sulzer Type 2 is one of the

Above:
Among the prototype catering vehicles employed at various periods was griddle car No E1106, the third vehicle of the 09.30 'buffet' from Cambridge, approaching Woolmer Green behind Class 31 No 5613 on 8 November 1973. The slow line tracks had recently been lifted, after repositioning of the junction with the quadruple track section. *David Percival*

Seven of the experimental vehicles — three open seconds, two corridor seconds and two corridor firsts — together with Mk I brake seconds and catering vehicles in matching blue and grey livery, ran in this diagram from 15 June until September. The set then transferred to the up 'West Riding' and 4.20pm to Leeds before moving to the Western Region in January 1965. The other 'Talisman' set, covering the down morning and up afternoon trains became a part-Pullman formation in June 1964, with four of the 1960-built Pullmans providing the first class accommodation. A similar formation replaced the 'XP64' stock on the 'Talisman' in September, but with four traditional Pullman Cars. The Pullmans were withdrawn from these trains in April 1965.

By early 1966, blue and grey coaches were appearing in ones and twos on most trains, but the first complete formation in the new livery was made up for one of the Newcastle/Edinburgh rosters, from 21 March.

Withdrawal of the Quad Arts had proceeded apace during the late 1950s and early 1960s and by the end of November 1965 only four sets remained — Nos 67, 74, 79 and 90. They covered three diagrams on Mondays to Fridays, as follows:

06.48 Baldock-King's Cross/17.40 Moorgate-Hertford/ECS to Hitchin/19.19 Hitchin-Baldock;

08.04 Welwyn Garden City-King's Cross/17.48 King's Cross-WGC;

08.25 Hatfield-King's Cross/17.20 King's Cross-Hatfield.

Set No 74 had been withdrawn by the beginning of April 1966 and the last three were towed north by a Class 31 on the morning of 2 April, *en route* to Sheffield and the breaker's yard. Replacements for the last Quad Arts were five-coach sets of non-corridor stock (formed S-S-BS-S-S), about 35ft shorter in length but seating only 504 compared with the Quad Arts' 648.

The demise of LNER main line stock meant that by mid-1967 it was rare to see even the final Thompson coaches in the area except occasionally on summer weekend-only services. Thompson sleeping cars, however, were included in the 'Aberdonian', and the unique Gresley 12-wheeled sleeper-first No E1677E, remained in use until early August. The first Pullman Car was observed in the new livery in July; No E320E on the 'Yorkshire Pullman'.

A new generation of main line stock was ushered in during the autumn of 1967 when Mk IIa vehicles were included in an air-braked formation working the 07.25 Newcastle-King's Cross and 18.00 return from 27 November. Within three months the 07.55 down and 16.45 return was similarly equipped, as were four West Riding services in each direction.

From 1 April 1968, two more sets covered the four 'Talisman' services; other ECML expresses equipped during the year included the 09.00 and 11.00 departures to Newcastle.

At the end of 1968, three LNER buffet cars were in regular use — No E9130E in a Cleethorpes set, No E9195E on a Cambridge 'Buffet' and 1948-built buffet No E1705E working between King's Cross and Peterborough. Apart from buffet and sleeping cars, all LNER passenger-carrying stock was withdrawn at the beginning of 1969. At the same time, the LNER travelling post office vans were replaced by BR Standard vehicles on the 20.20 and 22.30 Edinburgh trains and corresponding up services. January 1969 saw a decline in the use of LNER sleeping cars, only Gresley No E1211E and Thompson No E1292E (both in blue and grey livery) being noted during the month. Even LNER parcels vans were scarce by the middle of the year and an observation of nine of them in the King's Cross area

on 26 August was noted in the author's records as 'the most in one day for many months'.

The beginning of the 1969/70 timetable, on 5 May, saw more air-braked trains introduced. By July there were 22 sets available, for 20 main line services in each direction on Mondays to Fridays. From May, second class accommodation in the 'Tees-Tyne Pullman' was provided by ordinary stock (as in the 'Hull Pullman' since October 1968) and a few months later ex-Scottish Region griddle car No 1102 appeared in the train.

LNER buffet cars were given regular main line work in May 1970 when Nos E1706E and E9122E were included in the two new 'Highwayman' trains. The latter was replaced by No E1705E in September.

The year 1971 was notable for the introduction of air-conditioned Mk IId stock on East Coast trains. A total of 210 vehicles was ordered, comprising 128 open seconds, 23 corridor firsts, 19 open firsts, 23 corridor brake firsts and 17 open brake seconds. The first batch entered service on 12 July in three diagrams:

07.45 King's Cross-Newcastle and 13.15 return;
11.00 King's Cross-Newcastle and 17.00 return;
07.35 Newcastle-King's Cross and 18.00 return.

From 23 August, the 13.15 from Newcastle turned round as the 19.00 to Bradford and three further diagrams commenced:

New vehicles were built for the car-carrying passenger services in 1962. *Below:* **The up 'Anglo-Scottish Car Carrier' includes 10 of the original vans as it approaches New Southgate behind EE Type 4 No D247 on 5 July 1961.** *Bottom:* **The same train on 22 June 1962 is newly-equipped with double-deck 'covered wagons'. It is hauled by No D243 and, after running through Finsbury Park on the slow line, is about to take the up goods line to Holloway car loading bay.**
BR, Eastern Region; David Percival

07.55 King's Cross-Bradford, 11.50 return and 15.55 King's Cross-Harrogate;

07.25 Leeds-King's Cross, 11.30 to Harrogate and 16.22 return;

07.15 Bradford-King's Cross, 12.20 to Hull and 17.40 return.

Anglo-Scottish trains, including the 'Flying Scotsman' and 'Talisman' were equipped with Mk IId stock in the autumn.

In the early 1970s the remaining LNER buffet cars were normally seen at King's Cross on excursion and other special trains. However, on 25 May 1973, No E9132E was included in the formation of the 16.10 (FO) to Newcastle and in December 1974 No E9115E temporarily replaced a standard vehicle in one of the Cambridge 'buffet' sets. The same car was noted in the 10.20 King's Cross-Leeds in November of the following year. In the spring of 1976, Nos E9131/2E were in action on excursion trains, as was Thompson buffet No E1706E, which made possibly the final visit of an LNER passenger vehicle to the 'Cross' at the end of the year.

For some years, the King's Cross outer suburban service had been the only user of locomotive-hauled non-gangwayed stock. During 1976/7 the last two seven-coach rakes were in action only during the morning and evening 'peaks', finally working the 07.13 Royston and 08.01 Stevenage-King's Cross and the 17.42 King's Cross-Royston and 17.46 to Hitchin on 30 September 1977. On the following

Monday these duties were taken over by Class 312 EMUs. The 14 coaches were stored at Welwyn Garden City and gradually departed until the last pair, composites Nos E43012/43, went in March 1978.

The introduction of HSTs in the early part of 1978 (see Chapter 12) began the final phase in the reduction of locomotive-hauled passenger stock. Yet there were still some innovations, including further types of catering vehicles: modified buffet car No E1883 was in ECML service that summer. Then, in the winter of 1980/1, the buffet and miniature buffet cars in the York, Hull and Cleethorpes sets were replaced by micro-buffet cars Nos E6601-9, newly converted from Mk IId open seconds. Actually they operated more frequently as open seconds than as buffets, especially since the catering service was somewhat less than predictable. One of the sets included Nos E6604/7 together for several weeks, during which time No E6601 also joined the formation!

Another version of the micro-buffet appeared in the summer of 1981, when Mk IIa rakes appeared at the 'Cross' for the first time in several years. A pair

Top:
Thompson first class sleepers built in 1950, Nos E1259/60E, were among the last LNER sleeping cars in ECML service. Marshalled together, they show both the compartment and corridor sides as they pass Harringay on their way out of the 'Cross' on the morning of 28 June 1967. *David Percival*

Above:
'Deltic' No 55.016 *Gordon Highlander* brings its train of Mk I sleepers to a halt as the late-running 20.15 from Aberdeen stops to set down at Stevenage on 11 April 1978. Commuters were more surprised by the snow than by the sight of a 'overnight' arriving in the middle of the rush hour! *David Percival*

of sets worked a two-day diagram involving the 07.23 Peterborough-King's Cross, 09.40 to Edinburgh and (on the second day) 09.10 Dundee-King's Cross. Micro-buffets Nos E6507/10/21, converted from Mk IIa open seconds, were noted on these services.

The long-awaited replacements for ageing Mk I sleeping cars arrived late in 1981 and a set of the new Mk III vehicles was made up for a press trip from Aberdeen on the night of 17/18 December. Introduction of the cars in public service was on the 'Night Aberdonian' of 10 January 1982. After the following night's run, however, a series of ASLEF one-day strikes caused sleeping car services to be withdrawn and normality was resumed only on 19 February.

Commencing in May 1982, the new timetable brought a number of changes to overnight services and to the formation of sleeping car trains. For three weeks some trains were formed of Mk III sleepers and Mk IId open seconds. Then, from 7 June, most services were revised to convey exclusively sleeping cars or ordinary stock. As the number of Mk III sleepers increased, more Mk I vehicles were taken out of service and the last were replaced — on the 01.00 to Newcastle and corresponding up train — in May 1983. The standard formation is eight sleeping cars with a full brake at each end, although some services also include two open seconds and extra vans, loading up to 14 vehicles in all.

At the time of writing (December 1983), the overnight services are the only locomotive-hauled Inter-City trains running to and from King's Cross. Three loco-hauled Mk I sets are in use on Mondays to Fridays, forming the 06.32 semi-fast from Peterborough and the return services at 17.08, 17.15 and 17.41 (with balancing ECS workings). All other daytime passenger services in the area are provided by HSTs, Class 312 and 313 electric units, and Metro-Cammell Class 101 2-car diesel units. Apart from the few remaining Mk I vehicles, two links with the coaching stock of 25 years ago — privately owned Pullman Car *Doris* (albeit from the 'Brighton Belle') and Mess & Tool Van No DE320899, converted from a Gresley corridor second — stand at each end of the station at Finsbury Park.

8

Moving the Freight

To sit by the lineside out of King's Cross today is to count on the fingers of one hand the number of freight and parcels trains. Evening and night-time observation will produce some freightliners and a little more freight and parcels traffic. How different it was 25 years ago.

In daylight hours a procession of long coal trains rumbled towards London and returning empties rattled northwards. 'Pick up' freights ambled along, calling at small goods yards — which most stations possessed — to detach or collect coal wagons, covered vans and cattle trucks. During the evening, a stream of fitted freights headed north into the dusk and darkness. On a day chosen at random from the author's records — Thursday 28 August 1958 — 32

Below:
New England 'WD' No 90154 appears to be making good speed with an up coal train on the fast line north of Stevenage about 1960. *D. Ludford*

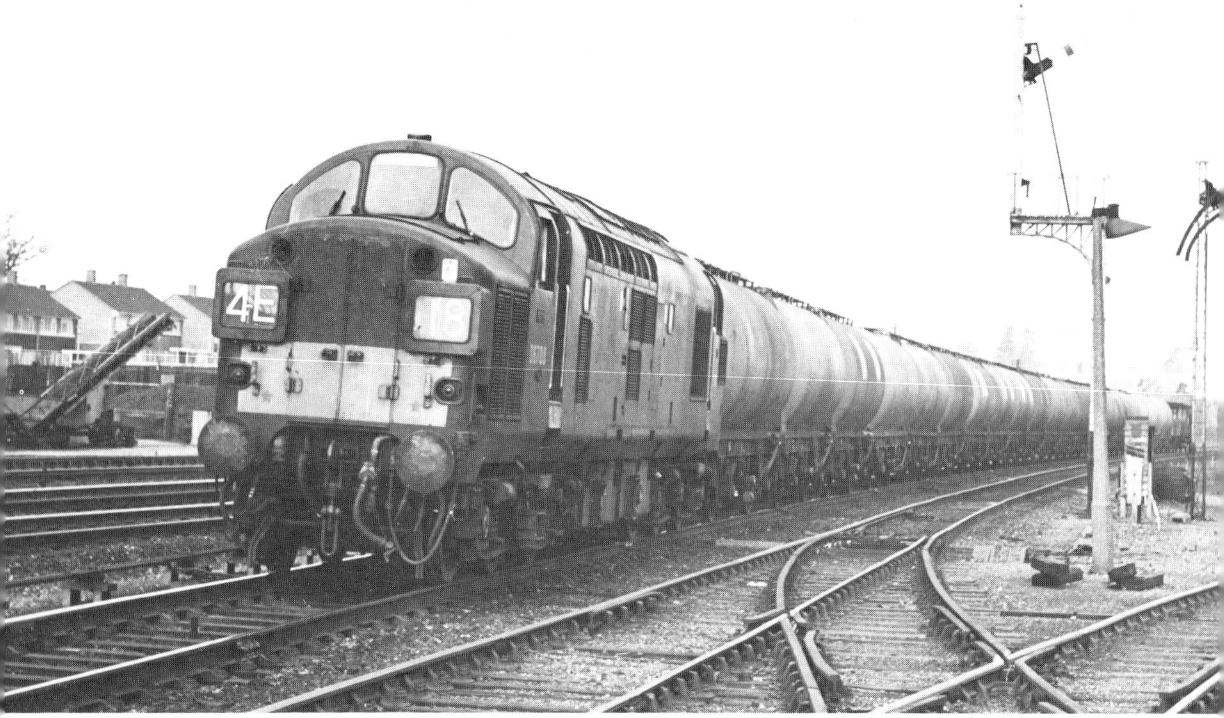

Above:
A Royston-Thames Haven empty petrol train approaches Oakleigh Park, with English Electric Type 3 No D6700 in charge, on 18 March 1967. *David Percival*

Right:
With bogie cement wagons in tow, a Class 47 accelerates the northbound Cliffe-Uddingston train after a pw slack at Welwyn North on 10 August 1974. Evidence of the forthcoming electrification is just beginning to appear. *David Percival*

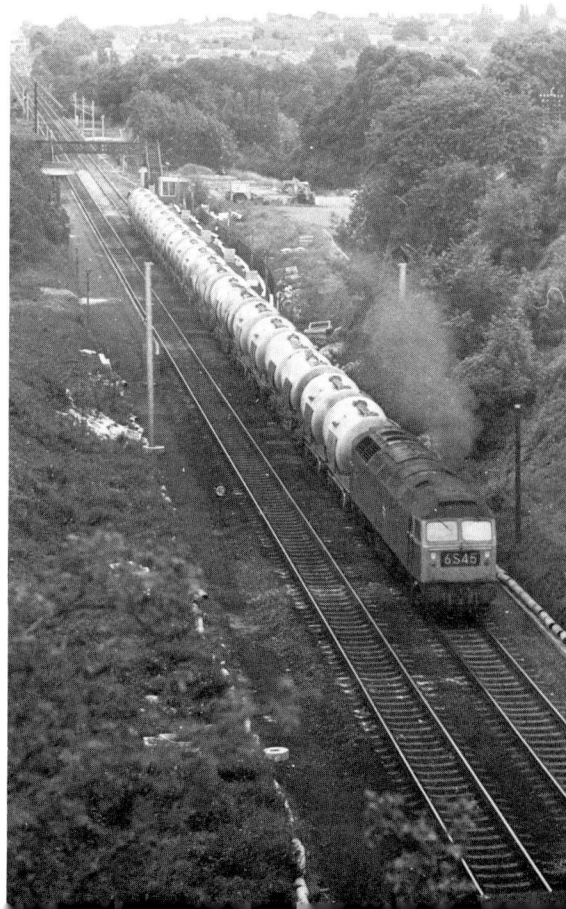

freight and parcels trains passed Knebworth between 9am and 9pm; several others would have been routed via the Hertford Loop.

The biggest yard in the area, Ferme Park, was a scene of constant activity, dealing with cross-London and transfer traffic as well as receiving and despatching main line freights.

The pattern of GN line freight movements was to undergo a dramatic change in the next 10 years. For example, the already declining fish traffic from Grimsby, Hull and Aberdeen was to disappear completely. In order to improve deliveries from the last-mentioned port, roller bearing axleboxes were fitted to a batch of the most modern vans in the late 1950s. Known as 'blue spots', from their prominent identification marking, the vans were rostered at the beginning of 1958 to the 12.30pm from Aberdeen and the return 'empties' from King's Cross Goods at 11.40am. One of the other fish trains — the 3.32pm Hull-East Goods — was of interest for its loco-

motive working. It was hauled throughout by a King's Cross 'B1' which had travelled down with a freight the previous evening; this was the longest through working for an Eastern Region 'B1'. During 1958, Top Shed's BR Class '5' 4-6-0s were occasionally employed on this duty, but a 'B1' was always preferred. Within a few years, these and other services were no more, and the last fish trains anywhere in BR ran in 1967.

But a determined effort was made in the early 1960s to capture more of the growing traffic in petroleum products, and 10-year contracts were signed with the major oil companies. In the King's Cross area a new oil depot was set up at Royston in January 1962 and this was supplied by trains from the LTS line, initially hauled by 'WD' 2-8-0s based at Tilbury (and sometimes proving a difficult task for a 'J20' 0-6-0). In later years these trains brought Stratford '37s', '47s' and '31s' to the GN line, the '31s' usually working in pairs (and the '37s' likewise for a period in the late 1970s). By 1969, Royston was handling two trains a day, each of 10 100-ton bogie tank wagons. A new domestic heating oil distribution depot at Watton-at-Stone was receiving one train a week at this time, and two trains of naphtha feedstock each day were running from Fawley to the Eastern Gas Board works at Cadwell, north of Hitchin. Another inter-regional working — between Lindsey, Lincs, and Langley, near Slough — also traversed the GN line with oil in the 1970s.

Motor car traffic was also a 1960s success story. From May 1964 three trains a week conveyed Ford vehicles from Dagenham to Bathgate, using one set of 22 carflats. An additional service, to Wakefield five times a week, was inaugurated in the following year. Extra capacity on these car-carrying trains was provided by the articulated double-deck vehicles known as 'Cartic-4s', which were introduced in 1965.

Among the earliest 'block' company trains was a Blue Circle haul from Purfleet to Leith and Cambuslang, which commenced in 1960 and carried cement in Presflo wagons. From August 1961, a twice-weekly Blue Circle cement train commenced running between Cliffe, on the Isle of Grain, and Uddingston, on the outskirts of Glasgow. At first a pair of BRCW Type '3' diesels brought the train to Ferme Park and a '9F' worked forward but from the beginning of December, when the train was running daily, the Type 3s worked through to York and returned with the empties. In later years a single

Type 3 was employed. These trains were formed of new Cemflo tank wagons, designed for cement traffic. By the end of the decade the trains had reverted to Eastern Region motive power for their journey over ECML metals and had been re-equipped with bogie cement tank wagons. The trains ceased running in October 1976.

While oil and other traffic increased during the 1960s, coal declined, though with some interesting developments. After trials in May 1958, a proportion of coal traffic was conveyed in '9F'-hauled trains of brake-fitted wagons for a time, but difficulties with the brake equipment and couplings brought an end to this experiment. Also in 1958, a mechanised domestic coal distribution depot — the first of its kind — opened at Palace Gates and was fed by trains, originating at Mansfield, of 18 21-ton hopper wagons emblazoned with the Charringtons legend. A similar depot was installed at Enfield Chase in September 1962 and the consequent closure of coal and other depots in the vicinity brought workings to an end on the Edgware and High Barnet branches at the beginning of October.

In April 1963 the number of coal trains and heavy freights between New England and Ferme Park was reduced by the introduction of a new '7 star' freight train classification (numerical classifications had

Below:
Coal for the home fires is worked down from Ferme Park by 'N2' No 69587, approaching New Southgate on 16 April 1960. *N. H. Willoughby*

Above:
One of the series of evening freights from London approaches Harringay behind 'K3' No 61805 on 24 June 1961. *C. T. Gifford*

Below:
'B1' No 61302 takes the slow road through Biggleswade with an up freight on 20 October 1962. *R. F. Orpwood*

replaced alphabetical train headcodes in June 1962). The Eastern Region plan was to reduce the number of categories from seven to two ('4' and '7 star'); in the event, classes 6, 8 and 9 were retained. On '7 star' trains, with the extra braking power of a 'head' of fitted vehicles on trains of more than 30 wagons, the load was limited not by what the locomotive could stop (as with class 7) but by what it could haul at a steady 35mph. Brush Type 4s were rostered for the trains and were able to take up to 90 wagons

(including a fitted head of 16), compared with a maximum of 75 on a Class 7 unfitted freight hauled by a '9F'. The result was fewer trains and more predictable running times.

The main change in coal traffic came in the middle of the decade. Coal from Yorkshire was re-routed to the Midland line or via the ex-GN/GE 'joint' line and the GE to London. At the same time, express freights to and from the north were concentrated on the ECML, some of them running from Stratford via

Eastern, Southern and Midland Region 0-6-0s on inter-regional freight duty. *Above:* 'J6' No 64253 takes the spur down to the Tottenham & Hampstead line at Harringay. Hornsey's 'J6s' were transferred to New England early in 1960 after the English Electric Type 1s arrived. *Above right:* 'Q1' No 33021 at Harringay in 1961 on a working from the Southern Region. *Right:* '3F' No 43808 waits at Hitchin to return with a freight to Bedford on 21 April 1962.
D. I. D. Loveday (2); R. F. Orpwood

Canonbury and Finsbury Park, and Ferme Park's role as a cross-London interchange yard began to be phased out.

It is perhaps curious that, on a line noted for its express passenger services, some of the most acclaimed services of the late 1950s and early 1960s were freights. The Hull fish and Cliffe-Uddingston cement have already been mentioned, but the best-known of all was train number 266 — the mid-afternoon King's Cross-Niddrie. In 1956 it had been retimed to run non-stop to York, and became part of a Top Shed lodging turn to Newcastle. Normally an immaculate 'A4' (or sometimes an 'A1') headed the train until EE Type 4s gradually took over from 1961 onwards.

In a period when certain express freights received names, the 8.10pm King's Cross-Newcastle service, introduced in June 1960, was entitled 'Tees-Tyne Freighter' and the name 'King's Cross Freighter' was

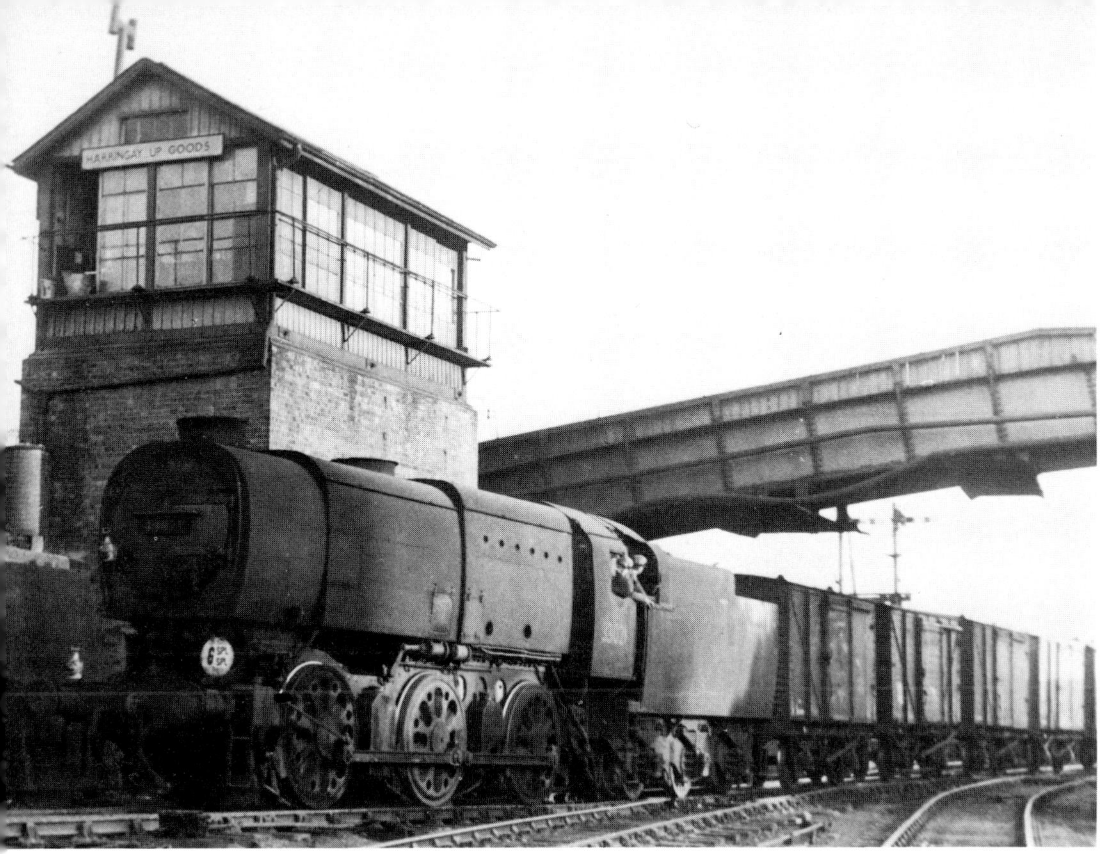
HARRINGAY UP GOODS

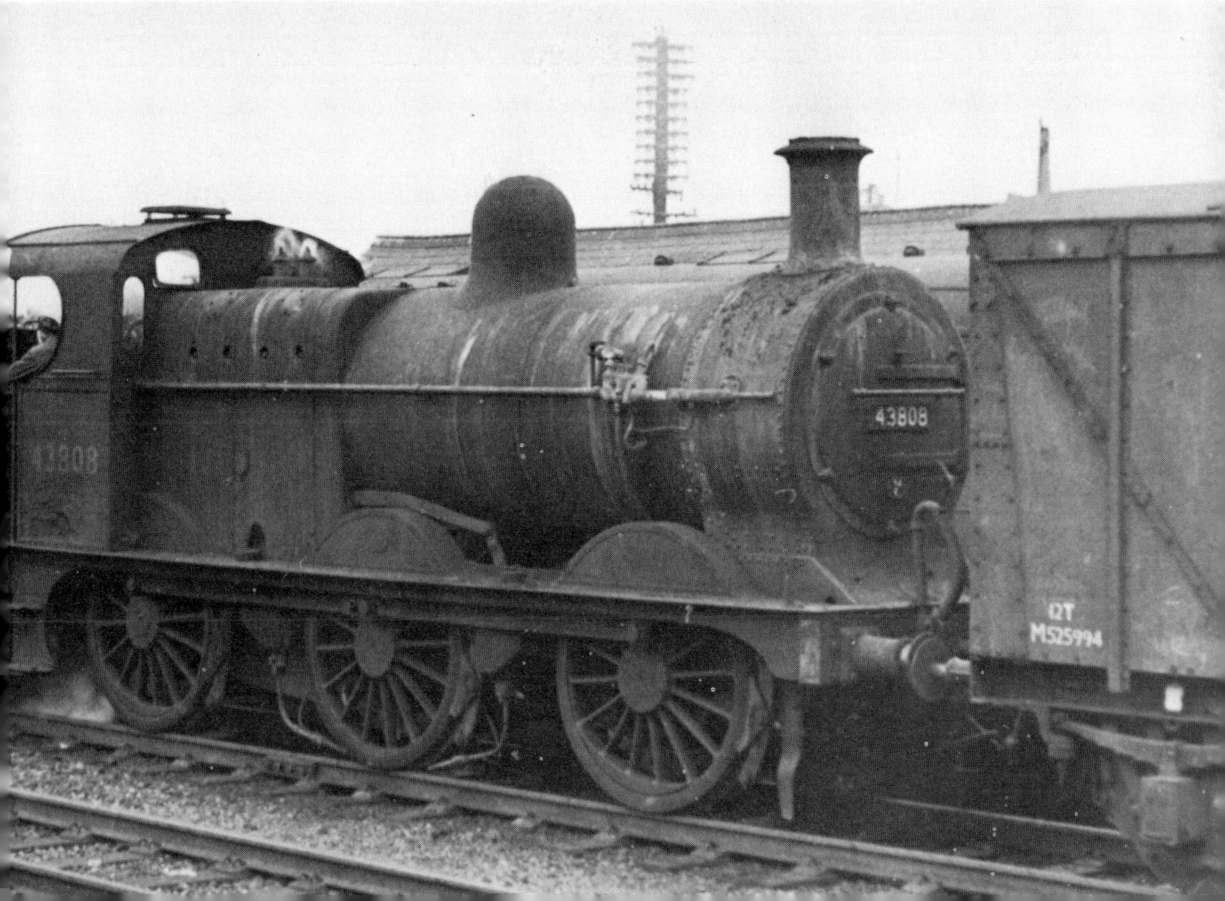
43808
12T
M525994

bestowed upon the corresponding up train. Locomotive headboards were prepared and attached for publicity photographs, but were subsequently used rarely, if at all.

In the spring and summer of 1963 a series of trials was held with the Roadrailer train, between Enfield Chase (where the train was stabled) and Doncaster. The Roadrailer, as its name implies, was adaptable for both road and rail use and had achieved some success in the USA. Each vehicle was equipped with alternative road and rail 'back axles'; on the road it was basically an articulated trailer and on rails the front end was supported by the axle assembly of the vehicle ahead. The intention was to start a King's

Cross-Newcastle-Edinburgh service in August but this was thwarted by a coupling breakage on one of the final trial runs. After modifications the train took to GN metals once more a year later, but the project was later abandoned.

The battle to come to terms with competition from road transport continued with the Freightliner. The first to operate on the East Coast main line, from 31 October 1966, was the 18.35 King's Cross-Aberdeen and 11.50 in the reverse direction (reaching London at 23.35). Within a year there was also a Sheffield service and three from Stratford, gaining the ECML at Finsbury Park and running to Leeds, Stockton, and Newcastle. During the early

Above:
EE Type 1 No D8049 shunts the yard at Letchworth during a 'pick up' freight working on the Cambridge branch in the early-1960s. *P. Ingarfill*

Right:
Class 37 No 6831 opens up approaching Three Counties with the Leeds–Tilbury freightliner in 1971. The train was frequently powered by a Stratford '37', although Class 47s were also employed. In 1972 the train was re-routed via the 'Joint' line and the GE. *D. J. Rice*

Top:
Class 37s worked the Fen Drayton–King's Cross sand train for many years until May 1983 when pairs of Class 31s took over the duty. No 37.090 heads the train between Ashwell and Baldock on 31 March 1983. *David Percival*

Above:
During the summer of 1959, Doncaster '9Fs' frequently worked the 6.35pm Clarence Yard–York parcels. One of them, No 92198, tops up its tender from Langley troughs. *D. Ludford*

Below:
In October 1982 the 20.15 and 22.30 King's Cross–Edinburgh 'mails' were shorn of their passenger accommodation. Now reduced to two BGs and two TPO vehicles, the 20.15 passes Oakleigh Park behind Class 31 No 31.242 on 5 July 1983. *David Percival*

1970s, Stratford and Willesden assumed greater importance as London's freightliner terminals. In 1972 only the Aberdeen train ran from King's Cross, but freightliners routed via the GN line included a Willesden-Leeds service and others running between Stratford and Leeds, Newcastle, Edinburgh and Glasgow.

Throughout the upheaval in the pattern of freight traffic, parcels trains had remained virtually unchanged, but a reorganisation of this traffic took place late in 1967. Specially allocated vans, lettered 'Parcels Express' were rostered to trains to and from Peterborough, Boston, Sunderland and Edinburgh. Most of the vans were BR Standard GUVs, but each train included a Gresley BG repainted in all-blue livery to accommodate the guard.

After the withdrawal of LNER parcels vans, followed by those of the other 'Big Four' companies' designs, parcels trains assumed an even more uniform appearance and are now formed only of BR Standard BGs and GUVs. The decline of freight traffic included the closure of Royston oil depot at the end of 1982, although in May 1983 Sherriffs of Hatfield took over the terminal for grain traffic, which is also handled at Sandy. Sand trains to King's Cross and Alexandra Palace and a daily working of vans to Kellogs' distribution centre at Marshmoor are the only other regular freight flows into the area but during 1983 a Section 8 grant was awarded towards provision of a rail-connected warehouse and distribution terminal in the old goods yard at Welwyn Garden City.

Above:
Brush Type 4 No D1514 heads the test train of 51 Roadrailer vehicles south of Cuffley on 25 April 1963.
BR, Eastern Region

Below:
A Bathgate-Dagenham service of empty 'Cartics' and loaded carflats passes Hitchin behind Class 47 No D1102 on 19 July 1969.
J. H. Cooper-Smith

9

Locomotives of the 'Park'

British Rail's first purpose-built main line locomotive maintenance depot was built on the site of the former Clarence Yard goods depot, on the west side of the line south of Finsbury Park station. It was opened in the spring of 1960, and the official locomotive transfer list shows 69 main line diesels and 17 diesel shunters moving from Hornsey on 24 April to 'Finsbury Park Diesel Loco Maintenance Depot (Clarence Yard)'. The depot was coded 34G at the beginning of 1961 and FP in 1973.

The depot consisted of a single-ended shed with six roads, each capable of taking three large locomotives, with provision for carrying out maintenance at high and low levels on all tracks. Facilities were

available for periodical examination and repairs, as well as daily servicing. The yard included stabling sidings and was provided with fuelling and sanding points. Workshops, stores and offices were adjacent to the rear of the locomotive shed.

The initial allocation was made up of six English Electric Type 4s Nos D201/6-9/48; 16 BRCW Type 2s Nos D5304-19; 24 Brush Type 2s Nos D5586-5609; 10 'Baby Deltics' Nos D5900-9; 13 EE Type 1s Nos D8020-7/45-9; and 17 0-6-0 diesel shunters Nos 12112/29/31/7/8, 13331/2, D3691-3, D3704-6/10-3. The first new locomotives, Nos D5610/11, were officially allocated on 28 April. Consequent upon the arrival of Brush Type 2s, the BRCW locomotives were beginning to be transferred to Scotland (Nos D5300-3 went early in April). A total of 54 Brush Type 2s was allocated at the end of the year and, although this was exceeded once or twice, their numbers remained at around the 45-55 level for the next 17 years.

Below:
Class 40 No 40.159 at the fuelling point on 25 February 1978. On the left is 'Deltic' No 55.012 *Crepello*; Nos 55.004/5/7 and a Class 47 are standing outside the depot. *D. J. Rice*

Locomotives of more than a dozen types, including shunters, were allocated to the 'Park' over the years, some continuously — like the Brush Type 2s and 'Deltics' — and others for brief periods only. A brief summary of the various main line types follows.

Paxman Type 1 (Class 15)

The first of a small allocation, No D8237, was delivered in November 1960. By the end of February 1961, Nos D8210 (transferred from Stratford) and D8238-43 had also arrived. The class was employed on local freight duties and weekend engineering trains, but achieved moments of glory on passenger work in an emergency. On 17 May 1962, for example, No D8240 was observed at New Barnet waiting to work the 8.20am to King's Cross, and on 15 June 1964 No D8231 powered the 5.52pm Moorgate-Hatfield. Early in 1969 the 17.08 Broad Street-Potters Bar was hauled by Class 15s on at least two occasions; on 6 March the locomotive was then commandeered for the 17.10 King's Cross-Cambridge after a Class 31 failed at Hadley Wood. A shortage of motive power saw the Paxmans working ECS to and from King's Cross in February 1964.

An allocation of about half-a-dozen remained throughout the 1960s, though the locomotives themselves were transferred to and from Stratford from time to time. Every locomotive from No D8229 to D8243 was at Finsbury Park at one time or another, as were Nos D8201 (for a short period in 1970) and D8210. The last pair, Nos D8231/2, were transferred away in December 1970.

Four members of the class — three of them formerly based at Finsbury Park — were converted to train heating units upon withdrawal and renumbered

DB968000-3 (ex-D8243/33/37/03). One came to the area in 1971 for use at Holloway carriage sidings but by 1975 all four could be seen during a journey from King's Cross to Wood Green — normally two at Holloway, one at Hornsey or Bounds Green and one spare on Finsbury Park depot. The units were later replaced by electric train heating units converted from Class 31s.

English Electric Type 1 (Class 20)

Employed mostly on freight and some empty stock workings, the EE Type 1s were among the most reliable locomotives allocated to Finsbury Park. They proved to be useful stand-ins for summer passenger work during the troubles with the 'Baby Deltics' in 1962/3, having already covered some passenger duties north of Hitchin and on the Dunstable branch in previous years. The 6.43am Royston-King's Cross in the summer of 1962 was regularly hauled by a 'thousand horse', which galloped along on the non-stop stretch from Knebworth to Finsbury Park, often completing the $22\frac{1}{2}$ miles in three or four minutes less than the booked 29min.

The allocation remained fairly constant during the years, No D8020 moving to Darnall at the end of April 1960 and returning in September 1962, and No D8021 doing the same in May 1962 and March

1963; Nos D8022-24, however, did not return after their transfer to Darnall in May 1962.

In 1964/5 the Type 1s appeared less frequently on passenger services, but an unusual working in December 1965 was the use of a Type 1 piloting a Brush Type 2 out of King's Cross on the 18.17 to Peterborough on several occasions. The last substitution by an EE Type 1 on a passenger train was almost certainly that of No D8027 working the 06.48 Baldock-King's Cross after a 'Baby Deltic' failed at Letchworth, on 12 April 1966, then continuing in the diagram to work the 09.04 Cambridge 'buffet'. Five days later, the class left the area when Nos D8020/1/5-7/45-9 were transferred to Immingham.

English Electric Type 2 (Class 23)
The 10 'Baby Deltics', Nos D5900-9, were uniquely associated with the King's Cross area — specifically with Hitchin, where they were normally based. During the first part of their career they were widely used on outer suburban passenger services, including several of the daily 'Cambridge Buffet Expresses'. By the winter of 1961/2, serious engine failures saw them taken out of service one by one and stored at Stratford Works. The last succumbed in June 1963,

by which time thought was being given to fitting them with conventional diesel engines. In July 1964, however, No D5904 returned from Vulcan Foundry with a modified Deltic engine, four-character headcode panel and new livery. The rest of the class followed in the next nine months.

Once more their forté was outer suburban passenger work, but now they were to be found more frequently on inner suburban duties. By 1968, recurring problems again took them out of service and the first was withdrawn in October of that year. All except Nos D5905/9 (the latter was the only one to receive blue livery) were withdrawn by the end of 1969. The remaining pair soldiered on until February and March 1971.

BR/Sulzer Type 2 (Class 24)
A suitable locomotive for cross-London freight working was at last found in the BR/Sulzer Type 2 after trials with No D5094 at the end of 1960. In the

early months of 1961, Nos D5050-72/94/5 were transferred from March and Stratford to Finsbury Park. Their main duties were inner suburban passenger services — including Dunstable branch trains — and ECS workings. Notable exceptions were the 7.35pm Ferme Park-Westwood (Peterborough) fitted freight which was entrusted to a pair working in multiple in 1962, and a Saturday outer suburban trip on the 8am to Baldock and 9.51am return in 1964.

Late in 1965, Nos D5053/4/72 returned from overhaul at Derby in the two-tone green livery then being applied to new BR/Sulzer Type 2s. In the following August, Nos D5057-72/94/5 were transferred to various depots in the Midland and Scottish Regions; Nos D5050-6 remained until October when they too went to Scotland.

BR/Sulzer Type 2 (Class 25)
For short periods, two of the 1,250bhp BR/Sulzer Type 2s were on loan to Finsbury Park, No D7526 for two weeks in May/June 1965 and No D7600 for seven weeks in August/September 1966.

Birmingham RCW/Sulzer Type 2 (Class 26)
The 16 BRCW/Sulzer Type 2s which came from Hornsey when Finsbury Park opened were in the process of being transferred to the Scottish Region. All but three departed by the beginning of July; Nos D5318/9 went at the end of September and the last to leave was No D5311 in mid-October.

Brush Type 2 (Class 30 and 31)
During 1960 the number of Brush Type 2s rapidly multiplied, thanks to a delivery rate of two a week. Including those transferred from Hornsey, Finsbury Park had received Nos D5586-99 and D5600-15/39-54/72-9 by the end of the year, although No D5587 had already moved on and the others up to No D5605 were exchanged for BR/Sulzer Type 2s early in 1961. The Brush Type 2s were the only main line diesels to operate from Finsbury Park throughout its 21 years' existence as a maintenance depot. They were employed on virtually every duty

during that period — from King's Cross station pilot to Pullman trains, from 'pick up' freights to freight-liners.

In the early months an occasional titled train duty was on the 1pm 'Heart of Midlothian' as far as Peterborough, returning with the 'Northumbrian'; Nos D5612/3 performed this duty in multiple on 17 May 1960 only two or three hours after arriving new! In the early 1960s they shared in the working of Sheffield Pullman services and in later years they were frequently employed, singly or in multiple, on Cleethorpes, Leeds, York, Hull and Newcastle expresses. But they were best known for their suburban passenger work and in the 1970s they were the mainstay of the locomotive-hauled services.

Replacement of the original 1,365bhp Mirrlees engines by 1,470bhp English Electric engines commenced with No D5677, one of the Finsbury Park locomotives, in March 1964, and the rest of the class were similarly modified between 1965 and 1969. The Mirrlees-engined locomotives became Class 30 in the 1968 reclassification and the others became Class 31. A later variation was the sub-division into '31/1' and '31/4' — the latter for locomotives equipped for electric train heating in the early 1970s, distinguished at Finsbury Park (and later copied by other depots) by their white-painted waist strip in 1978/9.

Over 110 different Class 31s were allocated to Finsbury Park at one time or another, of which a few are worthy of special mention. Allocated from May to July 1962, No D5835 with its engine uprated at 2,000bhp worked the main line diagram on which most of the prototype diesels were employed, commencing with the 8.10am departure. The first

Below:
Apart from five weeks away on loan, Class 31 No 31.189 served at the depot longer than any other main line locomotive. As No D5612, it stands at the down platform at Winchmore Hill with a permanent way train on 25 February 1968. The locomotive is in green livery with the BR 'arrow' symbol and new-style numerals. *Graham S. Cocks*

example without a headcode panel based at the depot was No D5552, which arrived at the end of March 1965 and remained until June. That summer, Nos D5671-4 were fitted with tablet-catching apparatus for working on the single-line Highdyke branch, south of Grantham.

When main line locomotives were transferred away at the end of May 1981, 16 '31/1s' and eight '31/4s' went to Immingham, March and York. Nos 31.191/217-9/22/407/8 had spent their entire careers to that date at Finsbury Park. However, No 31.189 (ex-D5612), allocated from new on 5 May 1960, can justifiably claim the record for the longest stay, notwithstanding its five-week loan to the Midland Region in February/March 1965.

Birmingham RCW/Sulzer Type 3 (Class 33)

Locomotives of this type were on loan to Finsbury Park on two occasions in 1961, for a few days each. In order to test its electric train heating equipment, No D6504 made two trips along the ECML after arriving with its eight-coach train from Derby on 10 February. The first left King's Cross at 12.30pm on 14 February and ran to Craigentinny, returning at 12.10am next day to arrive at Hornsey some 9hr later. The run was repeated on 16 and 17 February and the train returned to Derby on 20 February.

For a week before through working to York of these locomotives on cement trains began, on 4 December 1961, No D6559 came to Finsbury Park and made a number of crew training trips with empty coaching stock within the suburban area.

English Electric Type 4 (Class 40)

The six Type 4s transferred from Hornsey were the only examples of the type allocated to Finsbury Park and remained for little more than a year. In June 1961 Nos D201/6/7 moved to Stratford, and No D248 returned to Gateshead a month later. The remaining pair, Nos D208/9, were retained during the summer for the Sheffield Pullman workings and also worked the 10.30pm 'sleeper' as far as Newcastle, returning with the 'Tees-Tyne Pullman', until they too were transferred to Stratford. In November 1966, No D208 returned to Finsbury Park for a month, and No D201 also spent a month based at the depot from mid-January 1967.

BR/Sulzer Type 4 (Class 46)

Immediately prior to delivery of 'Peaks' to the East

Coast main line, Finsbury Park had No D154 on loan for four months from mid-February 1962. Its usual duty was the Doncaster-and-back diagram commencing with the 8.15am from King's Cross. No D155 followed for a brief spell in July and August and, in 1965, No D174 was also on loan for a few weeks in the early summer.

Brush Type 4 (Class 47)

At the end of September 1962, No D1500 arrived; after a month of occasional trips on the 8.10am departure it went to the Western Region for a further month of trials. In the New Year, Brush Type 4s took over some of Top Shed's Pacific duties but at the beginning of April 1963 they were switched to working express freights and the new '7 star' heavy coal hauls and returning empties between Ferme Park and New England. The first 20, Nos D1500-19, had provision for ETH, but the equipment was not fitted until required in the early 1970s. This batch had a long association with Finsbury Park and several were allocated continuously until 1979, apart from two years at Immingham in 1968/9. The largest number was allocated in 1965/6, when almost 50 (mostly in the D1500-50 series) were on the books.

In later years, Finsbury Park maintained around 20 Class 47s, mostly '47/4s', but Nos 47.009-11 came from Stratford in May 1980 — complete with grey roof panels, which Finsbury Park wasted no time in painting over! Dispersal of the dozen remain-

Above:
The 08.48 from York passes Holloway carriage sidings on 22 March 1973. Its Class 47, No 1508, was allocated to Finsbury Park from new in January 1963 until transferred to Gateshead in August 1979, apart from a spell at Immingham from November 1967 until October 1969. *Brian Morrison*

Right:
'Deltic' No D9018 *Ballymoss* is just a year old as it waits to depart with the 10.45pm to Leeds on 16 November 1962.
Anthony A. Vickers

ing when the depot closed in May 1981 was: Nos 47.162/549 to Stratford; No 47.422 to Immingham; and Nos 47.423/5/6/8-31/57/8 to York.

English Electric Type 5 (Class 55)

The long partnership between Finsbury Park and the 'Deltics' commenced when No D9001 was delivered in March 1961. Within a year the stud was complete — Nos D9001/3/7/9/12/5/8/20, all named after 'Classic' race winners. The allocation was to remain constant except for the addition of No D9021 (from Haymarket) in the first half of 1965 and the exchange of Nos D9001/3/9/12 for Haymarket's Nos D9000/13/6/9 during the first six months of 1968, to concentrate air-braked locomotives at Finsbury Park.

An interesting comparison was made at the end of 1963 when the depot's 'Deltics', with a total service of $18\frac{1}{2}$ years, had amassed a mileage of some 2,850,000 miles. The oldest 'A3' Pacific still in action, No 60106, had run $2\frac{1}{2}$ million miles in 40 years.

Always the best turned out 'Deltics', Finsbury Park's examples widened their reputation in the final years when they worked excursions and railtours over new metals. The distinctive white cab roof was first applied to No 55.003 in the spring of 1979 and

Nos 55.007/9/12/5/8 were similarly treated within a few months. But Nos 55.001/20 had been in Doncaster Works since March and April 1978; after some 18 months of rumours they became the first of the class to be withdrawn, at the end of 1979.

On the last day of Finsbury Park's existence as a traction and maintenance depot, Sunday 31 May 1981, the last daytime express worked by a Finsbury Park 'Deltic' was the 16.05 King's Cross-York, for which No 55.009 was given the depot's special external treatment and adorned with a headboard proclaiming 'Farewell Finsbury Park'.

The final farewell to the 'Park' came after a further $2\frac{1}{2}$ years as a servicing point for locomotives working into the area. At the beginning of October 1983, the remaining Class 08s were transferred to Bounds Green, where visiting main line locomotives are now serviced. Finsbury Park depot was handed over to the Divisional Civil Engineer's Department.

Below:
The down 'Flying Scotsman' approaches Finsbury Park behind Class 55 No 9001 *St Paddy* **on 8 February 1970. Western Sidings DMU shed can be seen to the right of the locomotive.** *J. H. Cooper-Smith*

10

Specials and Emergencies

Steam traction, with its attendant facilities, ended in the King's Cross area too early for the multitude of unusual locomotive workings which were a feature of mid-1960s 'specials'. But homegrown locomotives provided some memorable moments, the most stirring of them on 23 May 1959, when the partnership of Bill Hoole and 'A4' No 60007 took the Stephenson Locomotive Society Jubilee special to Doncaster and back. The train reached 100mph three times, including a maximum of 112mph on the return journey.

On 26 April 1958, a Pullman observation car was on the rear of the all-Pullman 'Pennine Limited', which departed from King's Cross on the first leg of its itinerary behind 'A1' No 60157. The train was organised by the publishers of this book, as were a pair of 'spotters' specials to Doncaster Works in April 1960. Preserved 4-4-0s No 3440 *City of Truro* and the Midland Compound No 1000 set out on 20 April but the GWR veteran was removed with a hot-box south of Peterborough on the return trip, leaving the Compound to return unaided. The 'City' was not available six days later and No 1000's partner was the last 'B12' in service, No 61572.

Locally preserved 'J52' No 1247 was active in 1961, working a brake van special over the Hatfield-St Albans branch on 17 June and two more outings in September. In its last year of service, 1962, 'A4' No 60022 *Mallard* was a popular choice for special duties. It headed an Ian Allan special to Doncaster on 26 April and the first leg of the RCTS/SLS 'Aberdeen Flyer' (the last non-stop King's Cross-Edinburgh working of an 'A4') on 2 June. In addition it took part in Crusader specials on 11 and 18 April and worked a Pullman charter to Harrogate and back on the first weekend of May. The LCGB 'Great Northern Railtour' of 19 May went to Doncaster behind 'A3' No 60066 and returned behind 'A4' No 60017.

A few days before the end of steam in 1963, an impressive visitor to the 'Cross' was LMS Pacific

No 46245 — immaculate in maroon livery — taking enthusiasts to Doncaster and back and 9 June. Four weeks later, the first official breaking of the ban on steam allowed 'A4' No 60007 into the terminus to work the LCGB 'Mallard Commemorative Railtour' — again to Doncaster and return on 6 July.

Two 'A3s', Nos 60106 and 60051, were used on railtours on 2 May and 6 June 1964, respectively, and No 4472 *Flying Scotsman* worked out of King's Cross for the first time since being preserved, on 30 August and 3 October. More variety was seen that autumn when 'Britannia' No 70020 took a special to York on 4 October, and 'A4' No 60009 worked the 'Jubilee Requiem' to Newcastle and back on 24 October.

During the 1960s, No 4472 was a familiar sight at the 'Cross', reaching a peak of about 10 special workings in each of the years 1967 and 1968. Its second tender was seen for the first time when it took the 'Elizabethan' special to York and back on 22 October 1966. On the previous day — and in order to work the 'Elizabethan' forward to Newcastle — 'Merchant Navy' Pacific No 35026 travelled light engine through the area on its way to York. It returned to London about three hours after the special on 22 October.

Another *Flying Scotsman* trip, on 2 June 1967, coincided with a second — though unconnected — steam locomotive working; in the early hours of that morning, preserved 'A4' No 4498 *Sir Nigel Gresley* travelled up light engine on its way to a special booking on the Southern Region. Preserved 'K4' 2-6-0 No 3442 *The Great Marquess* had come south light engine for the same reason in March. A bonus for enthusiasts that autumn was the series of clearance trials made by GWR 4-6-0 No 7029 *Clun Castle*, before working specials to Leeds on 17 September and York on 8 October. It was probably the only Great Western locomotive ever to use the turntable at Hitchin's former steam shed when it was turned there during these visits.

Right:

Preserved 'J52' No 1247 approaches Hertford North after working an enthusiasts' special over the branch from Welwyn on 16 September 1961. The train has just passed beneath the viaduct carrying the line from Wood Green. After withdrawal (as No 68846) in May 1959, the 'J52' was restored to Great Northern livery and preserved at Marshmoor; in February 1965 it departed under its own steam for a new home on the Keighley & Worth Valley Railway. *B. Coles*

Below:

From 1964 until 1969 *Flying Scotsman* was a frequent visitor to the 'Cross'. On 30 April 1967 it worked a special to Chesterfield and, after running on the slow line, accelerates away from Cadwell, north of Hitchin, on the down fast. *David Percival*

Above:
After arriving from Ballater behind an 'A1' on 16 September 1961, a Royal Train crosses to the down side at Hitchin, hauled by 'A3' No 60044 *Melton*, which was waiting to take the ECS northwards. In the event, the stock had to return from Biggleswade to Hitchin and head north again as a Royal Train.
D. Ludford

Right:
With an LMR electric unit in the background, the 'Inter Suburban' Cravens DMU special of 30 October 1976 waits to depart from Broad Street. The train travelled over all the existing suburban routes between London and Royston; it did not, of course, reach the destination temporarily shown on its indicator panel! *David Percival*

The event of 1968 was a non-stop special to Edinburgh on 1 May, the 40th anniversary of the first non-stop 'Flying Scotsman' express, when *Flying Scotsman* successfully repeated the run it had first made in 1928. A curious lapse was that of the following day's *Times* newspaper, which failed to acclaim the achievement. Instead, it stated that the train 'had to make three halts to take on water'. Had the 'Thunderer' not recorded Mr Ramsbottom's invention of the water trough?

During the year, No 4472 began to use Finsbury Park depot as its overnight 'base' instead of Hornsey, where it had previously stabled. The last of its visits to the 'Cross' before its North American trip, was on 31 August 1969 when — with warning bell already in place — it worked a return special to Newcastle.

In the steam era, Top Shed provided special trains of all kinds with immaculate motive power — none more so than in the case of Royal Trains, of which there were several in 1961. A sparkling selection of Pacifics was prepared on 8 June for the wedding of the Duke of Kent at York. Guests were conveyed in trains hauled by 'A4s' Nos 60003/15, followed by No 60028 on the Royal Train. Stand-by locomotives were Nos 60014 at King's Cross and 'A3' No 60067 and a spruced up New England 'A2', No 60514, — at Hitchin. Later the same month, No 60003 came up with the Royal Train returning from Corby on 19 June, and No 60033 worked a Royal special to Newcastle and back on 27 June. Hitchin was the focal point of another Royal Train working on 16 September. That occasion was notable for the sight of a spotless Gateshead 'A1', No 60147, bringing the train from the north, as well as for the fact that the stock eventually returned north as an unplanned Royal Train instead of working empty back to Wolverton.

In the late 1950s, the pantomime season brought a crop of outings to London for the children of employees of large firms in Stevenage and Letchworth. Generally a 'B1' headed the train, decorated with a smokebox-sized circular headboard. For the 'ICT Children's Party' on 9 January 1959, however, the 15-coach special required the services of 'V2' No 60871. Top Shed's 'B1s' were turned out for other short-distance special workings, such as the 'Hertfordshire Holiday Express' excursions to Hunstanton, Skegness, Yarmouth and Wroxham in the last week of July 1958 and 1959, and for Newmarket race specials. The latter were taken over by Brush Type 2s in 1961 but ended in the early 1960s.

A sporting event which continues to bring a large number of supporters' specials to King's Cross is the Rugby League Cup Final — as long as one or both finalists are from Yorkshire or Humberside! In the late 1950s, Heaton and Gateshead 'V2s' were seen in London on the trains, but 'A1' and 'A3' Pacifics gradually took over as their own regular main line duties decreased. Since 1963, Class 40, 46 and 47 locomotives have normally been in charge, although at least three EE Type 3s, based at Hull Dairycoates,

came up for the Hunslet v Wigan Final in 1965. In recent years, the Hull v Hull Kingston Rovers meeting in 1981 required a particularly intensive service from the Humberside city, while in 1983 an innovation was the use of the up yard at Welwyn Garden City for stabling five trains of stock between their incoming and return workings on 7 May.

Still in sporting vein, the pigeon specials which, until the 1960s, came to the London area from the North of England are worth remembering, not least for the length of the trains. Often hauled by 'V2s' from one of the Tyneside depots, they included a 19-vehicle formation on 25 June 1960 which arrived behind Gateshead named 'V2' No 60964 and returned behind another 'namer', No 60835 of Heaton.

Special workings in the diesel era have produced few unfamiliar locomotive types, although Southern Region Class 33s deserve a second glance when they appear occasionally on excursions to Spalding or on football specials. On 20 November 1976, however, the 'Western Talisman' railtour brought a diesel-hydraulic locomotive into King's Cross for the first and, to date, only time; Class 52 No D1023 *Western Fusilier* took the train to York and back.

Diesel multiple-units of various types have penetrated the area on special workings, including

Above:
'Deltic' No 55.002 *The King's Own Yorkshire Light Infantry* passes Drayton Park with the 'Deltic Fenman' of 4 May 1981, heading for the North London line and then via the Great Eastern to the Nene Valley Railway. No 55.002 had been repainted green the previous December. *Les Bertram*
Above right:
'V2' No 60885 lies derailed after its Leeds–London freight was unluckily involved in a collision between

two empty coal trains at Hitchin on 19 November 1958. Equally unfortunate were the crew of 'L1' No 67785, which was standing on the up slow and is now on its side beneath the pile of wreckage on the left. Happily, none of the railwaymen suffered serious injury. *B. Coles*
Right:
LMS Pacific No 46245 *City of London* passes Stevenage on 9 June 1963, returning from Doncaster with a special it had worked from King's Cross earlier in the day. *D. Ludford*

Hastings express sets, Derby 'heavyweight' units (Class 114), and Swindon 'cross-country' sets (Class 120). A special formed of two Cravens twin units was organised jointly by the Herts County Council Railway Society and the Stevenage Locomotive Society, and ran within the area on 30 October 1976, one week before introduction of the inner suburban electrified service. Sporting a headboard, the 'Inter Suburban' covered all the existing suburban routes to Royston — the only time this was achieved in a single itinerary, it is believed. A week later, a Class 31-hauled RCTS special traced a similar route but remained within the inner suburban area. The same society ran a Cravens DMU special via Hertford to Cambridge and Peterborough, and returned main line to King's Cross on 8 January 1978, a month before the outer suburban electric service began.

Electric multiple-unit specials ran on Jubilee Day, 7 June 1977, when fare-paying passengers travelled

Above:
Withdrawn two years earlier, but purchased for preservation, 'B12' No 61572 approaches Harringay with the 'Wandering 1500' railtour on 5 October 1963. The aptly-named special took the 'B12' to Stratford-upon-Avon. *D. A. Bosomworth*

Right:
'A4' No 60009 *Union of South Africa* speeds through Knebworth with the RCTS/SLS 'Jubilee Requiem' on 24 October 1964. Its return from Newcastle that evening was the last appearance of an 'A4' at the 'Cross'. *David Percival*

for the first time by electric train from Hitchin and other stations in the outer suburban area, in two six-car '313s' to Moorgate. Six and 9-car Class 313s conveyed fans from London to Stevenage for music festivals at Knebworth Park in the summer of 1978; previously the special trains had been formed of two six-coach non-gangwayed sets hauled by Class 31s.

The trappings of electric traction had appeared in the area in the late 1950s, when electric locomotives built at Doncaster for the Southern Region (later Class 71) were delivered via the East Coast main line. One of them, No E5002, made a striking contrast on 24 February 1959 when it was hauled southwards by ex-works 'N2' No 69581. At the same period, new diesel shunters (later Classes 03, 04 and 09) also passed through on their way to the Southern Region. The smaller shunters were often towed by a 'WD' or '9F' in an unfitted freight or coal train.

The first of the Doncaster-built West Coast locomotives, No E3056 (later 85.001) was towed up to London by '9F' No 92042 on 25 September 1960, for display at an exhibition of electric traction at Battersea.

From 1966 until 1974, a constant procession of new SR electric units built at York came south. Commencing with 4TC, 4REP and 4VEP units for the Bournemouth line, deliveries continued with 4BIG and 4CIG units and, finally, the later VEPs. At first, SR BRCW Type 3s went north to collect the units but, by 1969, Eastern Region Type 4s were bringing them to stable at East Goods, Ferme Park or New Southgate, where they were picked up by Class 33s. Some withdrawn Southern units were seen heading north along the ECML during this period.

On 10 August 1978, APT motor coach No Sc49003 was towed south with two test coaches by Class 45 No 45.116; the three-coach cavalcade returned north a week later behind Class 31

Special trains organised by the publishers of this book brought two preserved Great Western visitors to King's Cross in the 1960s. 4-4-0 No 3440 *City of Truro* piloted Midland Compound No 1000 on an excursion to Doncaster in April 1960, but failed on the return journey; it has two BRCW Type 2s for company *(Left:)* at Hornsey shed. In September and October 1967, No 7029 *Clun Castle* worked specials to Leeds and York; the latter *(Below:)* approaches Brookmans Park on 8 October. *D. I. D. Loveday; C. Green*

The Highgate branch from Finsbury Park was used for transferring London Transport tube stock between sections of the Northern Line. This working, on 7 October 1969, is from Drayton Park to Highgate, with the motive power provided by LT battery locomotive No 21. *Peter Foster*

The first electric passenger train from Hitchin calls at Stevenage on its way to Moorgate on Jubilee Day, 7 June 1977. The train was chartered by a local newspaper and was formed of units Nos 313 013/09. A BR '313' excursion followed a few minutes later. *Adrian White*

No 31.411. The visit of No 45.116 was something of a numerical coincidence; on 9 August 1961 — 17 years earlier almost to the day — Stanier 'Black Five' No 45116 had arrived on the overnight parcels from Newcastle.

Late in August 1978, a Wirral & Mersey Class 503 electric unit found its way to Hornsey electric depot for tyre-turning and remained for almost a month. The depot has also been visited by new Class 315 units for the GE, on several occasions in 1980/1, as well as older Eastern Region units — Nos 218 and 508 were present on 12 December 1980.

The summer of 1978 saw the first of several 'Deltic'-hauled special trains which ran until the class was withdrawn at the beginning of 1982. On 20 May 1978 No 55.012 took the outward leg of the 'East Coast Pullman Salute' marking the end of ECML Pullman services. Two BR excursions — to Skegness on 13 August and Lowestoft on 3 September — were hauled by No 55.015; the working of a 'Deltic' to unaccustomed destinations was featured in the publicity material. In 1981 three specials took 'Deltics' to the Nene Valley Railway, via the GE (returning direct), and the end of the year saw more 'Deltic' railtours from King's Cross or Finsbury Park. Last of all was the 'Deltic Scotsman Farewell' on 2 January 1982.

A trio of specials celebrating *Flying Scotsman's* 60th 'birthday' early in 1983 brought the SLOA Pullman set into prominence at King's Cross. On successive Sundays from 27 February, No 47.158 *Henry Ford* headed the 'Flying Scotsman' to Peterborough, where No 4472 itself took over. The same '47' hauled the Pullmans on two mid-week special workings early in March. King's Cross welcomed the VSOE Pullman train the same month, when it was chartered to take buyers to the Harrogate Fashion Fair on 14 March, returning the following day.

During the summer, the SLOA Pullmans were based at Bounds Green, though they were more often seen running empty to and from other parts of the country for weekend use than working out of the 'Cross'. Rarely have they been upstaged by a diesel locomotive, but this was certainly the case on 31 July

Above:
Prior to introduction of push–pull working between Edinburgh and Glasgow, trials were held between Doncaster and Sandy. One of the locomotives used was EE Type 3 No D6700, which propels the train beneath the Cambridge–Bedford line flyover at the start of its northbound run at 13.50 on 14 February 1968.
David Percival

Below:
A 'Western' in 'Deltic' territory! Since preserved, No 1023 *Western Fusilier* heads the 09.25 King's Cross-York 'Western Talisman' through Welwyn Garden City on 20 November 1976. *David Percival*

1983 when the prototype Class 40 took the 'Hadrian Pullman' from King's Cross to Carlisle. Freshly repainted in green livery, No 40.122 — or perhaps one should say D200, which number it also carried — recalled, for the author, its first visit to the area on a test run from Doncaster 25 years earlier. The spectacle also evoked memories of Finsbury Park's English Electric Type 4s on East Coast Pullmans newly-equipped with the stock in 1961.

The word 'emergencies' in the title of this chapter signifies those out-of-course happenings which disrupt and delay traffic. Excluding failures of equipment such as locomotives and signalling, the three main causes are weather, accidents and industrial action. In the past quarter of a century the King's Cross area has had its share of all three.

Bad weather made itself felt on two occasions at the beginning and end of the period, heavy snow in February 1958 and December 1981 even resulting in trains being stranded on the line. On 24 February 1958, the 2.25pm to Cambridge, hauled by Standard '5' No 73157, stuck in a snowdrift between Ashwell and Royston and the 3.25pm Dunstable-Hatfield was similarly entrapped near Ayot. In both cases the line was blocked for 24 hours. Snow brought down the overhead line between Stevenage and Hitchin on

Above:
During its travels around the country, the 'Train Catering Centenary' special ran from Leeds to King's Cross on 13 September 1979. The drab appearance of Class 47 No 47.543 (even the BR symbol is missing) contrasts with the colourful train as it approaches Stevenage.
David Percival

In addition to the 'Flying Scotsman' Pullmans, 1983 saw several other notable specials. *Right:* **The VSOE Pullman train took buyers to the Harrogate Fashion Fair on 14 March; the train is passing Wymondley behind Class 47 No 47.415, whose condition caused some adverse comment in the northern press.** *Below right:* **Immaculate in its new green livery, re-instated Class 40 No D200/40.122 passes Knebworth on its way to Carlisle with the 'Hadrian Pullman' on 31 July.** *Both: David Percival*

Left:
'9F' No 92192 was not the first locomotive — nor the last — to end up in this way after running through trap points on the down slow before the double-track section at Arlesey. The 2-10-0 had been working the 7.50am Clarence Yard-Hull freight on 22 October 1958. *D. Ludford*

13 December 1981 and one of the Hertford-Letchworth '313s' was marooned until the next day.

A train abandoned in the snow is somewhat alien to the King's Cross commuter, who is more accustomed to an event usually occurring on a weekday in July or August, just before the evening 'peak' — The Annual Flooding of Gasworks Tunnel! In fairness, it seemed as if the problem had finally been overcome in the late-1970s, but a freak downpour on 9 July 1981 isolated King's Cross once more and, for a few hours, Finsbury Park became the southern terminus of the East Coast main line.

Fortunately, most of the accidents which have occurred in the area since the beginning of 1958 have resulted in minor injuries only to train crews and passengers. Such was the case on 19 November 1958, when a '9F' on a Ferme Park-New England haul of empty wagons ran into the rear of a similar train on the down fast line south of Hitchin, in thick fog around 4.30am. Almost immediately, an express freight from Leeds collided with wreckage on the up fast line and its derailed vans overturned an 'L1' standing on the up slow. Although the down slow was clear about seven hours later, it was not until 8am next day that all four tracks were open again. Main line trains were diverted via Peterborough and Cambridge to Liverpool Street or Stratford and outer suburban services ran to or from Stevenage.

Similar main line diversions (though running to and from King's Cross via Hitchin) were in operation for almost two days following a freight train collision at Offord on 7 September 1962. Class A1 No 60123, hauling the 8.50pm down Leeds freight, ran into the rear of the 8.25pm freight to Aberdeen and was so badly damaged that it became the first member of the class to be withdrawn.

Hatfield was the scene of two incidents early in 1966. On 12 January the last three coaches of the 17.27 King's Cross-Cambridge derailed and slew across all but the up slow line at the north end of the

Above:
Class 31 No 5624 ran through stops and down an embankment at Hertford North in the early hours of 17 February 1971. The photograph was taken that evening and the locomotive was hauled back to rail level two days later. *David Percival*

station. Passengers in the crowded train had a lucky escape from serious injury. A few weeks later, on the morning of Sunday 20 February, Wrestler's Bridge, just north of the station, collapsed while deep reballasting of the up fast line was being carried out. Services were diverted via Hertford and, although the bridge was demolished and cleared by the Monday, it was not until 22 February that the up fast was relaid.

Tragedy struck at the same spot on 23 March 1968, when the 03.00 Temple Mills-Welwyn Garden City freight was unable to stop in the down goods road. Seeing what was happening, the signalman

tried in vain to reset the route back to the down slow but the locomotive, Class 31 No D5622, ran into the retaining wall at the end of a siding and the driver and secondman both died.

In the exceptionally hot weather of July 1969, the down 'Tees-Tyne Pullman' derailed at speed south of Sandy on 23 July, due to distortion of the continuous welded rail. Remarkable good fortune favoured passengers in the rear part of the train as the Pullman Cars scattered and overturned; only one person was slightly injured, others escaping with cuts and bruises only.

February and March 1971 saw several minor incidents, in the first of which '31' No 5624 ran through stops and down an embankment at Hertford North in the early hours of 17 February. Eight days later, '40' No 263 derailed at Letchworth while working a Whitemoor-Hitchin freight; '31s' Nos 5613 and 5644 were involved in a head-on collision in the sidings at Welwyn Garden City on 5 March, and the 13.05 from Newcastle hit the stops at King's Cross on 14 March.

Since the early 1970s, disruptions have tended to result from industrial action as much as from other causes. In some cases a local problem has been the cause (for example, a maintenance supervisors' dispute resulted in the cancellation of some main line services for about a week in April 1975); in others, such as a month-long ASLEF 'work to rule' starting in mid-December 1973, the action was national.

Unofficial action by locomen in March 1976 resulted in the unusual sight of 'Deltics' Nos 55.004/7/9/15 and '47' No 47.428 stabled for several days in a suburban platform at the 'Cross'. The 'Deltics' themselves were the subject of a dispute in October 1977 and, for a week, no members of the class were in action.

A series of three-days-a-week ASLEF strikes in January and February 1979 was one of the more damaging events, and a similar campaign was carried out three years later. That year also saw a 15-day 'flexible rostering' strike by ASLEF in July. Only a handful of trains ran to and from King's Cross each day, including some DMU services to and from Peterborough and Doncaster, bringing Lincoln and Hull-based units to London. All in all, 1982 was the year which suffered most from industrial action, with virtually all traffic lost on 32 days, not to mention the cancellation of overnight services and disruption on days before and after the one-day strikes.

_11_

Electrification

Among the many promises of King's Cross suburban electrification, dating back even to Great Northern days, was a forecast in 1958 by the then Line Traffic Manager, Gerard Fiennes, that electric trains would be running by the mid-1960s. When that date approached, the Divisional Manager of the day predicted '1970 or soon after'. In the event, it was not until August 1971 that authorisation was received for electrification to Royston, at a cost of £35 million. The inner suburban service was to employ dual-system multiple units, operating from Moorgate, via the Northern City line (then operated by London Transport) to Drayton Park, thence by means of a new link to Finsbury Park and on to Welwyn Garden City and Hertford North. Outer suburban trains would run from King's Cross to Royston, with a DMU connection to Cambridge. Eastern Region services to Broad Street and via the Widened Lines to Moorgate would come to an end.

Electrification work was to evolve in stages, linked to a broader programme of resignalling and track improvements between King's Cross and Sandy,

Above:
Battery electric locomotives on the crossover at Moorgate on 14 November 1975.
BR, Eastern Region

Right:
Class 313 No 313 002 on the 14.30 Moorgate-Hertford North service at Crews Hill on 7 August 1977.
Martin Higginson

Right:
Class 313 No 313 002 on the 14.30 Moorgate-Hertford North service at Crews Hill on 7 August 1977.
Martin Higginson

Below right:
A pair of Class 312 units, led by No 312 016, at Baldock on a down Royston working on 11 February 1978. The headcodes displayed when the units entered service had already been abandoned. *A. G. Merrells*

which was already under way. It was a tremendous project, leading to what would be virtually a new railway — and it had to be carried out while the existing services were running. A commendable public relations exercise was mounted to keep suburban travellers informed, by means of posters and free publications. The whole scheme was described in a booklet produced in 1973, and 12 issues of a progress report, *Livewire,* were published between 1974 and 1978.

Although track and signalling improvements were a priority, many signs of electrification were visible by the end of 1973. Bases for masts, the masts themselves and, in some places, overhead wiring had been installed in much of the inner suburban area north of Wood Green.

Above:
On 12 September 1973, Class 31 No 5638 takes the goods line flyover at Holloway, returning the electrification train to its base at King's Cross Goods. *Brian Morrison*

Progress accelerated during 1974, with bridges being raised and wiring reaching parts of the outer suburban area. South of Wood Green, track realignment was under way in 1975 and the new multiple-unit depot and electrical control room, on the site of Ferme Park up yard, was in the final stages of completion. In the vicinity of Kings Cross, a major construction was the rebuilding of the former up goods line flyover at Holloway, to bring electric trains from the up slow to the two platforms to be retained on the suburban side of the terminus. This was completed in May 1977.

The last London Transport train ran on the Northern City line in October 1975, by which time four battery locomotives (converted from Euston-Watford motor coaches) had arrived at Hornsey for working in pairs on engineers' trains in the tunnel section. By the end of the year the overhead line was energised on the Hertford loop and between Wood Green and Welwyn. Early in 1976 the first electric units came to Hornsey in the shape of LMR Class 312/2s and Great Eastern Class 312/1s, for commissioning and test trips.

Class 313 inner suburban units arrived at the end of March and went into service on 16 August 1976, operating on the 750V dc third-rail section between Drayton Park and Old Street only. On 8 November the full inner suburban service commenced. Since the fleet of 64 units was not yet complete, some rush-hour trains were formed of one unit instead of two until the early part of 1977, resulting in excessive overcrowding. During that time problems arose over the passenger-operated doors, with one or two cases of doors being opened while trains were on the move. This was resolved by removal of the passenger opening facility, and full control of the doors was taken over by the guard from March 1977. Passengers also experienced delays when up trains were terminated at Drayton Park and returned to Hornsey

Above:
Levelling, track-laying and mast-planting has already been carried out in the yard of the new electric depot at Hornsey on 12 September 1974. Five suburban coaches and a couple of wagons occupy the tracks that three years later will accommodate Class 312 and 313 EMUs. *Kevin Lane*

Below:
Wiring in progress on the down slow line north of Stevenage on 27 April 1975. About that time it was announced that all four tracks would be electrified north of Woolmer Green, instead of the slow lines only as originally planned. *David Percival*

after failure of the trip-cock mechanism on their train — or a false indication of failure given by the detector at Finsbury Park. When electrification was completed the solution adopted was to run the 'faulty' train into King's Cross instead of Moorgate.

On the positive side, the new service generated extra traffic; after 12 months an increase in season tickets of more than 30% over the previous year was reported, with new business as high as 160% from stations between Finsbury Park and Wood Green. The '313s' were kept remarkably clean externally by frequent washes (normally of plain water) as they entered the stabling sidings and, in this respect, set an example to some other operators.

Withdrawal of inner suburban services from the 'Cross' allowed the final reconstruction work to begin — a complete revision of the track layout between the station and Gasworks Tunnel (described

by ER publicists as 'clearing the Throat'), in which the easternmost of the tunnel's three double-track bores was to be abandoned. After suburban platforms 11-13 were closed at the end of 1976, the work was carried out in two stages over a period of nine weeks. Platforms 7 to 10 were out of action in February and 1 to 3 in March. During this time some commuter services terminated at the King's Cross York Road platform or started from platform 14, the empty stock reversing at Moorgate. In addition to routeing electric trains for platforms 9 and 10 over the Holloway flyover, two-way working on the four remaining tracks through Gasworks Tunnel was designed to further reduce conflict between arrivals and departures.

Early in 1977 the overhead line was energised as far north as Hitchin and tested by '313s'. The first of 26 outer suburban units, No 312 001, reached

Hornsey on 9 June and driver-training began without delay. Six units were delivered with the composite trailer at the north end of the train, but No 312 007 arrived the other way round and the others were turned to conform. By the middle of the year, King's Cross was ready to receive the electrics and, in September, inner suburban trains were diverted there more than once because of problems on the Moorgate line.

The first fare-paying passengers to experience electric traction in the outer suburban area were those travelling in two '313' specials on Jubilee Day (see chapter 10). On 28 September, some enjoyed

their first journey in a '312' between Stevenage and Royston after Nos 312 005/6 had made a demonstration run for the local press.

Class 312 units entered public service on 3 October 1977, when three diagrams were introduced, each for a pair of units. One six-car train ran ECS at 07.10 from Hornsey to Royston, then worked the 08.35 to King's Cross, 10.30 back to Royston and 12.44 return. The other pairs worked the 07.13 from Royston and 08.01 from Stevenage to King's Cross, and their evening duties were the 17.42 to Royston and 17.46 to Hitchin. More outer suburban workings were brought in a month later, including some weekend turns. On Boxing Day, with train services running for the first time since 1974, '313s' were employed on an hourly King's Cross-Hitchin service.

Below:
The 14.36 to Moorgate, formed of unit No 313 022, crosses the new flyover after leaving Welwyn Garden City on 21 January 1978. *Les Bertram*

Above:
Class 312 No 312 710 has just arrived at Royston as the 09.40 from King's Cross and No 312 725 is about to depart at 10.45 on 31 March 1983. *David Percival*

The full outer suburban electric service commenced on 6 February 1978, composed entirely of Class 312 units, apart from '313s' on the 00.20 Moorgate-Hitchin and mid-day and early evening 'mails'. In addition to the overall comfort, regularity and speed (with which some drivers took liberties in the early months), the '312s' brought a much-needed service to the outer suburban traveller. Their public address system means that passengers can now be kept informed about delays. Generally, guards explain the problem in a matter-of-fact way (though railway jargon sometimes confuses occasional travellers) but on one occasion the guard was clearly irritated. 'This *was* the 19.10 to Royston', he announced as the train departed several minutes late, due to delays on the up run which were caused by 'insipid signalling and regulating'. Smiles wreathed the faces of weary commuters, at that remark, as is the case with many of the ad lib comments. Among those heard by the author on down 'peak' journeys are 'enjoy yourselves' (after announcing a non-stop run to Stevenage); the helpful warning 'as we get out into the country the snow is falling, so take care when alighting'; the admonishing 'don't leave just

one glove behind — it will be no use to me'; and the greeting 'Happy New Year from myself and the driver' — which was somewhat ironic coming at the end of 1981!

As with the inner suburban electrics, delivery of Class '312' units was incomplete when the service started. It was late in 1978 when the last two, Nos 312 025/6, arrived — coinciding with the entry into traffic of the last '313', No 313 011. When delivered, No 312 025 was fitted with headlights, and the rest of the class was similarly equipped from September 1981. At the end of March 1979, the GN '312s' were renumbered 312 701-726. The last of the batch was transferred to the Great Eastern shortly afterwards and has subsequently been followed by inner suburban units Nos 313 008/34/5/9. During the latter part of 1983 Hornsey supplied six of its '313s' to the Midland Region while modifications were made to the St Pancras-Bedford Class 317 units.

12

The High Speed Trains

First sight of the High Speed Train in the King's Cross area was on 3 May 1973, when the prototype unit, then sporting an assortment of Mk I and test vehicles, ran from Darlington to Hitchin and back on a two-hour 100mph schedule. The unit reached Hitchin around 1pm and remained for some 90min. Its next appearance — and after creating a world diesel speed record of 143mph — was on 2 August. With seven intermediate Mk III coaches it ran from King's Cross to Darlington and back.

It was another two years before the prototype, now numbered 252 001, came to the GN line again. On 27 September 1975 it left King's Cross at 08.15 on a special working for the opening of the National Railway Museum at York. An electrical fire in one power car caused delay near Huntingdon and a stop at Peterborough. Returning that evening, the special passed through the outer suburban area 20min late but further problems resulted in an arrival over and hour behind time.

The first production HST to reach King's Cross was No 253 020, borrowed from the Western Region for a press demonstration trip to Peterborough at 10.40 on 26 April 1977. The actual time to Peterborough was 54min — 6min less than the fastest

Below:
The prototype High Speed Train is seen at King's Cross for the first time on 2 August 1973. The occasion was a high-speed trial run to Darlington and back.
David Percival

express timing at that date. Between Hitchin and Huntingdon the line speed limit was relaxed so the train could demonstrate its 125mph capability.

Another WR set, No 253 026, arrived in King's Cross around 14.30 on 13 June from Gleneagles, conveying heads of government returning from a conference. The same unit made the first King's Cross-Edinburgh HST run on 23 July, working the 'Silver Jubilee' enthusiasts' special out of the terminus at 07.40 and returning the same evening.

By the summer of 1977 the maintenance depot at Bounds Green was ready to receive its first units; No 254 001 came up on the morning of 12 September. At mid-day, four days later, No 254 002 arrived at Welwyn Garden City on a crew training trip, returning north after about half-an-hour. Included in its formation was the High Speed Track Recording Car No DB999550. The first outing of No 254 001 was to Selby and back on 29 September, a trip which was repeated several times in the following month. Crew training continued in November with No 254 004, then was stepped down for a month or so, during which time units Nos 254 004/7 were incongruously stabled in the old 'Coronation' carriage shed at Wood Green.

By the end of the year, new speed limit signs were in position beside the track, the first '125' out of King's Cross sited immediately north of Knebworth. Notices were placed at stations, warning passengers to keep back from the yellow line painted along the platforms.

In January and February 1978, pairs of power cars (and sometimes trios) shuttled to and fro, as did mixed formations of trailer cars hauled by diesel locomotives, with 'barrier vehicles' (Mk I and Mk II coaches) between the locomotive and the Mk III stock. Driver training, combined with demonstration trips for travel agents and BR staff, recommenced in February. The usual itinerary was King's Cross-York-Peterborough-Grantham-London. This gave two runs in each direction over Stoke and several drivers each day gained experience of braking from high speed at various locations.

The 125 era on the East Coast main line was launched on 20 March 1978. From that day the 07.45 Kings Cross-Edinburgh and 15.00 return was booked for an HST. The inaugural trip was made by a 'scratch' formation, with DMB No E43061 (of unit No 254 003) leading and No E43057 (of unit No 254 001) at the rear. The eight trailer cars were formed, from the north end: two TS, TRSB, two TS, TRUK and two TF. This remained the standard formation for the '254s' until May 1980 when the two catering vehicles were placed together between the first and second class sections of the train, to simplify supply and staffing arrangements.

On 4 April an all first class HST special ran from King's Cross via Cambridge to Norwich and back. Two TRUKs, Nos E40513/4, were among the eight coaches and the DMBs of No 254 010 provided the motive power. The 16.00 down 'Talisman' was worked by an HST for the first time on 3 May, pre-

Below:
South of Sandy in October 1978 is the 07.32 Newcastle-King's Cross, led by DMB No Sc43086. The train is as originally formed, with the buffet car in the centre of the second class section at the north end. *I. J. Hodson*

Bottom:
One of the DMBs transferred from the Western Region at the end of 1982, No 43044, receives attention inside Bounds Green depot in February 1983. On the right, buffet car No E1513 has been prepared for working with the SLOA Pullmans on the 'Flying Scotsman' specials. *Patrick Gosling*

saging more diagrams and the first accelerated timings when the new timetable commenced on the following Monday, 8 May. Eight workings each way on Mondays to Saturdays and five on Sundays were planned, mostly between King's Cross and Edinburgh but including some Newcastle services. Due to a shortage of units, two workings each way were locomotive-hauled for another two months and temporarily reverted to their previous schedules. On the first day the down and up 'Flying Scotsman' services were worked by Nos 254 001 and 254 007 respectively, with the train's title on a 'headboard' stuck beneath the cab windscreen. The units returned on the 'Talisman'; the up train, at least, retained its 'Flying Scotsman' identity as removal of the 'headboard' would have taken the paint with it!

An unusual incident involved one of the HST stock movements on the evening of 8 July. Due to late running of an up express, the formation of Class 31 No 31.322 hauling a barrier vehicle and DMB No E43063 was pressed into passenger service near Newark. It ran thus, calling at intermediate stations, to Stevenage where passengers transferred

from the barrier vehicle — a Mk I open first — to the Royston electric service.

Further diagrams introduced in the autumn of 1978 included the first to Aberdeen, from 2 October, on the 11.55 down 'Aberdonian' and 09.00 up. Formation changes occurred in December, when the two catering vehicles of some units were replaced by an unclassed buffet (TRUB) and an extra second class coach. The series of 34 units was completed in May 1979. Delivery of the two spare DMBs (Nos E43122/3) followed and within a few days both were observed in service on the same unit.

When the fully accelerated ECML timetable was introduced — delayed until the Penmanshiel diversion was completed in August 1979 — more new workings commenced. Among them were the 05.35 to Leeds, which replaced the 04.05 and reached Leeds 28min earlier. In October, the 10.45 Leeds-King's Cross reverted to locomotive haulage and was decelerated by 31min — a point which was lost on one 'Deltic' driver, who managed to arrive 30min early!

Complete failures of HSTs in the King's Cross area have been rare, although many are the times when a lineside observer is greeted by relative silence as one power car goes by. On 14 January 1980, however, the up 'Aberdonian' — delayed both by weather and failure — eventually reached King's Cross over five hours late, towed by Class 40 No 40.160. Several more instances occurred in 1983,

Below:
The now derelict signalbox at Potters Bar, built in 1955, remains a prominent landmark as another of the former WR power cars, No 43042, heads the 12.00 Edinburgh–King's Cross on 1 July 1983. *David Percival*

however, when the hot summer exacerbated cooling problems with the Paxman engines.

The years 1979-81 saw the transfer of all types of trailer from the Western Region, though most were later returned. This influx of vehicles proved useful during the summer of 1980 when some sets were increased to nine coaches (and designated Class 255) because of serious overcrowding on certain services. Developments in the winter of 1980/1 were the replacement of the north end TS by a trailer guard second (TGS) and delivery of the second series of '254s'. The power cars of these units, Nos 43153-62, were not equipped with a guard's compartment, and this provided another variation in appearance.

Two Hull return workings were taken over by HSTs on 1 June 1981, joining the 'Executive' which had been converted in January and leaving only one locomotive-hauled Hull service in each direction. Observation on that day showed that 30 sets were required for the services to and from King's Cross, with some covering three or four trains. One set worked ECS to Peterborough for the 07.40 to King's Cross, then the 09.35 to Newcastle and 14.30 return, and finally the 18.50 to Bradford. Once more, a 'headboard' was tried out on the 'Flying Scotsman' — and once more this resulted in the 'Talisman' travelling under an assumed name. In fact, DMB No 43104 carried the title for a week or more, which must have confused passengers heading for Leeds during that period.

The last months of 1981 saw units for the NE/SW service at King's Cross, as on 22 September when a formation with DMBs Nos 43167/8, branded 253 049, worked some Leeds services. The sight of unit numbers was by then unusual as most DMBs had lost the meaningless identification, the ECML authorities having long since decided that power cars were interchangeable. More appropriately, DMB numbers began to appear on coupler cover plates in the spring of 1982.

At the end of the 1981/2 timetable, one York and one Cleethorpes service in each direction were the only locomotive-hauled daytime InterCity services running to or from King's Cross. The York trains were handed over to HSTs in May 1982 and the Cleethorpes trains on 4 October. Thus the conversion of the ECML service at King's Cross was complete.

Below:
The driver can bring his train to full speed for the first time since leaving King's Cross as the 13.00 to Aberdeen passes the '125' sign at Knebworth on 1 July 1983. The rear power unit of this seven-coach formation, No 43118, clearly shows three external modifications made since the HSTs entered service — the cowling around the exhaust ports, designed to deflect exhaust and prevent stains on the cab roof and windscreen; the supporting strip for ladders enabling staff to clean windscreens; and the power car number which is carried on the nose of some units. *David Percival*

One of the later power cars without guard's accommodation, No 43160 (above right) heads an up express through Brookmans Park on 1 July 1983. On the same day, No 43085 *City of Bradford* (Right:) is the leading DMB of the 18.18 to Cleethorpes, restarting from Stevenage. The first of the original ECML power cars, No 43056, at that time un-named and with its distinctive black cab roof and number beneath the windscreen (Below:), leads the Sunday 14.10 from Newcastle on to the double-track section at Woolmer Green on 10 July 1983. Did someone say that all HSTs are alike? *All: David Percival*

The last of the original Western Region units, No 253 027, had already been reallocated to Neville Hill for 12 months when it was joined in October 1982 by Nos 253 022-26, together with spare DMB No 43121; another spare power car, No 43120, made the same move in January 1983 and later that year units Nos 253 019-21 followed. The introduction of HSTs on the St Pancras-Sheffield route in the winter of 1982/3 meant that the ECML was not suffering from an excess of units, as the Midland trains were provided by Bounds Green.

Developments in 1983 included minor livery changes. A black cab roof was sported by DMB No 43111 for a short time, on Nos 43106/7/14 the number was moved to a position just above the grille protecting the horns, and both changes were applied to No 43056 until its works visit in the autumn.

The trend for naming reached the HSTs when No 43113 became *City of Newcastle upon Tyne* on 26 April; three more quickly followed, including No 43153 *University of Durham*. By early 1984 names bestowed on power cars included newspapers, HST depots, a school and a regiment with ECML connections. The first six years of HST working was commemorated at Stevenage when No 43162 was named *Borough of Stevenage* on 21 March 1984.

Chronology

<table>
<tr><td colspan="2">1958</td></tr>
<tr><td>Apr</td><td>First main line diesel locomotive delivered to Hornsey</td></tr>
<tr><td>Aug</td><td>First DMU passenger train at King's Cross</td></tr>
<tr><td>Aug</td><td>First suburban diesel locomotive delivered to Hornsey</td></tr>
<tr><td>Sep</td><td>Introduction of 'Master Cutler' Sheffield Pullman service</td></tr>
<tr><td>Oct</td><td>Diesel-working begins on some inner suburban trains</td></tr>
<tr><td colspan="2">1959</td></tr>
<tr><td>Jan/
Feb</td><td>Three Counties, Arlesey, Offord closed to passenger traffic</td></tr>
<tr><td>Feb</td><td>Diesels introduced on outer suburban services</td></tr>
<tr><td>Feb</td><td>Prototype Deltic arrives for trials</td></tr>
<tr><td>May</td><td>Quadrupling through Hadley Wood/ Potters Bar completed</td></tr>
<tr><td>Jun</td><td>Diesel suburban timetable introduced</td></tr>
<tr><td>Dec</td><td>First Brush Type 2s (later Class 31) delivered to Hornsey</td></tr>
<tr><td colspan="2">1960</td></tr>
<tr><td>Apr</td><td>Finsbury Park depot opened</td></tr>
<tr><td>Apr</td><td>City of Truro and Midland Compound enthusiasts' special</td></tr>
<tr><td>Sep</td><td>New Pullman Cars introduced</td></tr>
<tr><td>Sep</td><td>Last steam-diagrammed suburban trains</td></tr>
<tr><td>Nov</td><td>Hitchin shed loses steam allocation</td></tr>
<tr><td>Dec</td><td>'Britannia' Pacifics introduced on Cleethorpes trains</td></tr>
<tr><td colspan="2">1961</td></tr>
<tr><td>Jan</td><td>Hatfield shed closed</td></tr>
<tr><td>Jan</td><td>Four-character headcodes introduced on suburban trains</td></tr>
<tr><td>Mar</td><td>First Class 55 'Deltic' delivered to Finsbury Park</td></tr>
<tr><td>Jul</td><td>Hornsey shed loses steam allocation</td></tr>
<tr><td>Sep</td><td>End of 'A4' working on 'Elizabethan'</td></tr>
<tr><td>Sep</td><td>First express accelerated to 'Deltic' timing</td></tr>
<tr><td>Oct</td><td>Prototype Falcon arrives for trials</td></tr>
<tr><td>Dec</td><td>BRCW Type 3s (later Class 33) begin through working to York</td></tr>
</table>

<table>
<tr><td colspan="2">1962</td></tr>
<tr><td>Jan</td><td>LMR Bedford-Hitchin passenger service withdrawn</td></tr>
<tr><td>Mar</td><td>Hertford-Stevenage passenger service re-instated</td></tr>
<tr><td>May</td><td>Last 'N2s' transferred out of the area</td></tr>
<tr><td>Jun</td><td>Introduction of Anglo-Scottish 6hr express timings</td></tr>
<tr><td>Sep</td><td>First Brush Type 4 (later Class 47) delivered</td></tr>
<tr><td>Dec</td><td>First 'A4s' withdrawn</td></tr>
<tr><td colspan="2">1963</td></tr>
<tr><td>Jan</td><td>'A3' No 60103 Flying Scotsman withdrawn for preservation</td></tr>
<tr><td>Apr</td><td>Introduction of Class '7 star' freights</td></tr>
<tr><td>Jun</td><td>LMR Pacific No 46245 works special to Doncaster</td></tr>
<tr><td>Jun</td><td>End of scheduled steam working south of Hitchin</td></tr>
<tr><td>Jun</td><td>Top Shed closed</td></tr>
<tr><td>Jul</td><td>Prototype No DP2 arrives for trials</td></tr>
<tr><td>Sep</td><td>Prototype Lion arrives for trials</td></tr>
<tr><td colspan="2">1964</td></tr>
<tr><td>Jun</td><td>'XP64' coaching stock introduced on 'Talisman'</td></tr>
<tr><td>Jul</td><td>'Baby Deltics' begin to return to service after modification</td></tr>
<tr><td>Aug</td><td>No 4472 Flying Scotsman works first special from King's Cross since preservation</td></tr>
<tr><td>Oct</td><td>Last appearance of an 'A4' at King's Cross</td></tr>
<tr><td colspan="2">1965</td></tr>
<tr><td>Apr</td><td>Luton/Dunstable branch passenger service withdrawn</td></tr>
<tr><td>Oct</td><td>Test run of 'Midland Pullman' from Leeds</td></tr>
<tr><td colspan="2">1966</td></tr>
<tr><td>Mar</td><td>First complete blue-and-grey train</td></tr>
<tr><td>Mar</td><td>Last Quad Art sets withdrawn</td></tr>
<tr><td>Oct</td><td>First Freightliner service from King's Cross</td></tr>
<tr><td colspan="2">1967</td></tr>
<tr><td>Sep/
Oct</td><td>Clun Castle works special trains</td></tr>
<tr><td>Nov</td><td>Introduction of air-braked coaching stock</td></tr>
</table>

1968

Jan	SR Hastings unit test run to Grantham
Feb	Push-pull trials between Doncaster and Sandy
May	*Flying Scotsman* non-stop special to Edinburgh
Jun	First 3-car DMUs (later Class 116) transferred to Finsbury Park

1969

Jan	LNER TPO vans replaced by new BR vehicles
May	Derby/BR DMUs (later Class 125) transferred to Finsbury Park
Aug	Last *Flying Scotsman* special before North American tour
Nov	Prototype *Kestrel* arrives for trials

1970

May	Low-fare 'Highwayman' service introduced (to Newcastle)

1971

Mar	Last 'Baby Deltic' withdrawn
Jul	Introduction of air-conditioned (Mk IId) stock
Aug	Electrification of suburban area authorised

1972

May	King's Cross platforms renumbered consecutively

1973

May	Prototype HST Darlington-Hitchin test run
May	Loco depots and stabling points recoded (FP, HI, KX)
Jun	New concourse and travel centre opened at King's Cross
Jul	New station at Stevenage opened
Aug	Test run of prototype HST King's Cross-Darlington

1974

Apr	First edition of *Livewire* published
May	'Executive' express titles appear in public timetable

1975

Jul	Battery locomotives arrive at Hornsey
Sep	Prototype HST King's Cross-York return special

1976

Aug	Electric service commences between Old Street and Drayton Park
Oct	Class 52 *Western Fusilier* special to York
Nov	Full inner suburban electric service commences

1977

Feb	King's Cross 'throat' remodelled
Apr	Press demonstration run of production HST
May	New flyover at Holloway brought into use
Jun	07.45 to Edinburgh and 15.00 return named 'Silver Jubilee'
Sep	Refurbished Metro-Cammell DMUs transferred to Cambridge

Sep	Last non-gangwayed loco-hauled coaching stock withdrawn
Oct	Electric units introduced on some outer suburban services

1978

Feb	End of through passenger service to Cambridge
Feb	Full outer suburban electric service commences
Mar	First HST introduced on ECML service
May	Last Pullman trains withdrawn
May	HST timings introduced on ECML

1979

Apr	First Finsbury Park 'white cab' 'Deltic'
May	Moorgate-Hertford-Letchworth service introduced
May	Down 'Hull Executive' accelerated to 91.3mph (to Retford)
Sep	Catering Centenary special, Leeds-King's Cross

1980

Jan	First 'Deltics' withdrawn (Nos 55001/20 of Finsbury Park)
Dec	'Deltic' No 55002 repainted green

1981

May	Finsbury Park loses main line locomotive allocation

1982

Jan	Last 'Deltics' withdrawn
Jan	Mk III sleeping cars introduced
May	Low-fare overnight 'Nightrider' service launched
May	Watton-at-Stone station re-opened
May	Wood Green station renamed Alexandra Palace
Oct	Last daytime loco-hauled InterCity service replaced by HST

1983

Feb/Mar	Series of *Flying Scotsman* Pullman specials
Mar	VSOE Pullman special to Harrogate
Apr	First HST power car named
May	Last Mk I sleeper services withdrawn
Jul	Class 40 No D200 (40.122) works Pullman special
Oct	Finsbury Park depot closed

Appendices

Appendix I
Steam locomotive allocation — 1 January 1958

King's Cross (34A) *Totals*

A4 4-6-2	60003/6-8/10/3-5/7/21/2/5/6/8-30/2-4	19
A3 4-6-2	60039/44/55/9/62/6/103/8/10	9
A1 4-6-2	60119/22/5/8/36/9/49/56-8	10
V2 2-6-2	60800/14/20/8/62/71/902/3/14/50/83	11
B1 4-6-0	61075/139/200/331/64/93/4	7
L1 2-6-4T	67757/68/70/3/4/9/84/93/4/7	10
J52 0-6-0ST	68831/62	2
N2 0-6-2T	69490-3/5-9/506/12/5/7/20/1/3/4/6-9/32/5/6/8-46/8/9/68-71/3-9/81/3-5/9/91-3	54
'5' 4-6-0	73157-9	3

125

Hornsey (34B)

J6 0-6-0	64196/223/33/53/66	5
L1 2-6-4T	67772/80	2
J52 0-6-0ST	68824/34/46/66	4
J50 0-6-0T	68891/4/903/6/7/17/8/20/1/8-31/6/45/6/9/61/6/8/71/2/9/81-3/5-7/9-91	32
N2 0-6-2T	69502/5/13/22/5/30/1/3/7/50-2/4-6/60/7/72/87/94	20
N7 0-6-2T	69618/29	2

65

Hatfield (34C)

J52 0-6-0ST	68867	1
N2 0-6-2T	69494/504/16/34/47/80/2/6/8	9
N7 0-6-2T	69631/2/5/7-40/4/8-50/4/704	13

23

Hitchin (34D)

B1 4-6-0	61027/90/1/3/4/7/105/251	8
J6 0-6-0	64175/86/97/206/37/40/51	7
J15 0-6-0	65479	1
L1 2-6-4T	67741/4-6/9/61/85/90/1	9
J68 0-6-0T	68638/54/61	3
N2 0-6-2T	69561	1

29

Note: In addition 31 350bhp 0-6-0 and four 204bhp
0-6-0 diesel shunters were allocated to the area.

111

Appendix II
Locomotive Allocation — 17 June 1963

Finsbury Park (34G)		*Totals*
Brush Type 4 Co-Co	D1500-26	27
British Railways 350bhp 0-6-0	D3307-12/31/2/4, D3692/3, D3704-6/10-8/22-5, 1211/29/31/8	31
BR/Sulzer Type 2 Bo-Bo	D5050-72/94/5	25
Brush Type 2 A1A-A1A	D5583/5, D5601-15/39-54/71-81	42
English Electric Type 2 Bo-Bo (1)	D5900-9	10
English Electric Type 1 Bo-Bo	D8020/1/5-7/45-9	10
BTH/Paxman Type 1 Bo-Bo	D8229-33/5/6	7
English Electric Type 5 Co-Co	D9001/3/7/9/12/5/8/20	8
		160

Hitchin (34D)		
British Railways 204bhp 0-6-0	D2000-3/18/9	6
Drewry 204bhp 0-6-0 (2)	D2235	1
British Railways 350bhp 0-6-0	D3128, D3687-91, D3708/9	8
		15

Notes: (1) All out of service — returned from July 1964
(2) From Colwick 16 June — transferred to Boston 30 June
(3) In addition 30 Cravens 2-car DMUs were allocated to Finsbury Park.

Appendix III
Motive power allocation — 3 October 1983

Bounds Green (BN)		*Totals*
Class 08	08.222/37/413/522/58/655/709/813/34/59/73	11
Class 254 DMB	43056/7/62/5/82-5/106/7/14/5/23	15

Hornsey (HE)		
Class 312	312 701-25	25
Class 313	313 001-7/9-33/6-8/40-64	60
Battery locomotives	97709/10	2

Front cover, top:
Two New England locomotives in full cry south of Hatfield on 20 October 1962. 'A3' No 60065 *Knight of Thistle*, working the 1.20pm Peterborough-King's Cross, overtakes an up coal train headed by 'WD' 2-8-0 No 90158. *C. T. Gifford*

Front cover, bottom:
Four High Speed Trains in almost perfect symmetry at King's Cross on the first day of the 1983/4 timetable, 16 May 1983. From left to right, the rear power cars are of the 12.04 to Hull, 12.50 to Leeds, 11.50 to Leeds and 12.00 to Edinburgh. *David Percival*

Back cover, top:
Flanked by BRCW/Sulzer Type 2s on ECS duties, 'A4' No 60006 *Sir Ralph Wedgwood* takes the 'Flying Scotsman' out of King's Cross on 27 November 1959. *Michael Joyce*

Back cover, bottom:
English Electric Type 4 No D249 waits to depart from Hitchin with the 19.45am Peterborough-King's Cross on 10 April 1965 as 'Deltic' No D9015 *Tulyar* approaches with the 10.20am King's Cross-Leeds. *David Percival*